The Ultimate Guide to Getting and Keeping Clients

BOOKED SOLID

BY PAUL J. DIGRIGOLI

Book design by Leslie Tane Design
Model Photos by Patrice Guyard
Photos of Paul by Edward Cohen

ISBN: 978-0-615-34932-9

First Printing

To my family, friends, students, and the DiGrigoli Team. Without question, I wouldn't have done it without you.

Contents

Introduction   1

1: Expectations &
    Getting Booked Solid   7

▶ Top 10 Tips   11

2: My Story   15

3: Why Be a Hairdresser?   25
▶ Case Study: Amanda   31

4: Clients: Without 'Em, You're
    Just a Person With Scissors   35

5: Evaluate Yourself   41

6: How to Be a Poor Stylist   47

7: How to Be an Outstanding Stylist   51
▶ Case Study: Jimmy   61

8: Personal Development   65

9: Motivation   79
▶ Case Study: Carlos   89

10: Marketing   93

11: Ethics   103
▶ Case Study: Angela   110

12: Achieve Your Peak State   115

Conclusion: Love What You Do
    & Expand Your Happiness   121

Acknowledgments   126

Introduction

I'm guessing that you bought this book to learn how to become a successful hairdresser. And I feel it's only fair to let you know that you are going to get much more than that. You see, I've learned that the way that you live your life and the way that you cut hair are inextricably linked. The success and health of one influences the other. So no, I'm not just going to show you how to become Booked Solid in the salon, I'm going to show you how to become Booked Solid in life; how to ensure that your 'chair' is always full of success, joy and passion.

Where am I finding you right now? At the beginning or in the middle of your career? In a time of great success or huge frustrations? Here's the thing: in the end, it doesn't matter. There's always room for improvement, for more, for greater success. This industry

Hairdressers can do what no one else can – not even a doctor. **We can make someone feel and look amazing in 30 minutes.**

is totally incredible, your options and your capacity for growth are endless.

I'm so glad that you're here. I've been a hairdresser for 30 years and in that time I've made mistakes, I've learned a ton, and I've had phenomenal success. It brings me great joy to share my experience and help others succeed, and I do this on a daily basis with my clients, staff, students and seminar attendees. I'm thrilled that now I can share it with you, too.

I wrote this book for two reasons:

#1. I WANT YOU TO SUCCEED, AND I KNOW YOU CAN.

I love what I do. I love my clients, I love my staff, and I love my students. I love making people look good and feel like a million bucks, and I love giving back massively. I love growing my business. And when you love what you do, it's never work.

I want you to love what you do as well. I want it so much, in fact, that I'm kind of anxious for you to start loving it immediately. A big part of you loving what you do depends on your level of success. Whoever you are and wherever you are in your life, you can be successful — I have no doubt.

Do you know how I know?

Let me ask you a question. Do you know why they make desks for 4th graders so small? Because at the end of the year, the 4th graders outgrow them and have to move on to the 5th grade. In other words, you're supposed to grow and make progress, year after year. If you're not growing, you're dying — life was designed that way. Be different, don't get stuck at the small desk.

So, here's the *big* question, how do you get from Point A to Point B? How do you grow and move on to the big desk?

It took me three decades to get where I am today. It's taken me 8 months to put everything that I've learned into this book. And it will take you about a week to read it. Do you know what that means? It means that this book will help you accelerate your learning. It will make the journey from Point A to Point B shorter and more efficient. It will give you measurable progress in a reasonable amount of time.

What could be better than that?

For me, it took 30 years, but my goal is to make sure that it doesn't take you that long. So, I'm sharing everything that I've learned with you. You won't have to make my mistakes...I made them for all of us.

#2. I WANT YOU TO AVOID FAILURE.

The second reason I wrote this book is because I know the top reason that hairdressers (or anyone, really) fail. It's simple. They fail because they get distracted.

Ray Kroc, the founder of McDonald's, once said, "As long as you're green, you're growing. As soon as you're ripe, you start to rot."

If you get distracted from your goals, your work, your vision, your life — that's when you turn ripe and rotten. The way to avoid that is to stay "green" — be interested, keep learning, stay focused. As a result, you'll keep growing, and you'll find more success and unlimited happiness.

What could be distracting you? The list is endless: boredom, physical health, drama at home, surrounding yourself with people who aren't driven to succeed — to name a few. You lose your purpose when you surround yourself with unhealthy distractions. The distraction could mean that you aren't learning the latest styles or new skills. Maybe you've stopped talking to clients or you show up to work late. Maybe you miss appointments completely. When you get distracted, you lose clients — and they'll take the money with them.

Being a hairdresser means being part of a relationship — with your clients, with your salon, with your colleagues, with your talent, with your continuing education. And like any relationship, if you stop paying attention to it, it won't survive.

I'm going to show you the road to avoiding distractions in this book. I would like to share with you how to fully engage for prosperity, health and happiness.

This is a great profession:

- Hairdressers can do what no one else can — not even a doctor. *We can make someone feel and look amazing in 30 minutes.*
- It's a 60 billion dollar a year industry. Women spend 12.5 million every year on color alone.

No matter how big the Information Age gets, no one will take our job. You could be walking down the street with a beautiful haircut and beautiful hair color and someone would stop you and ask, "Where did you get your hair cut?" You're not going to say, "Hey, I got it on the Internet". That will never happen.

Now, let's go get you a piece of the magic, the life you crave, and a hefty piece of that 60 billion dollar pie...

CHAPTER 1

Expectations & Getting Booked Solid

When your clients come to you for a haircut, they expect a few things.

They assume you'll be there, for starters. That you'll wash their hair, hear what they want, and then cut and style it just so. In return, you expect them to show up for their appointment, tell you what they need, sit straight in the chair, have some great conversation, and then pay you for the service.

Fulfilling these expectations puts you on the track to becoming booked solid.

HERE'S WHAT YOU CAN EXPECT TO GET FROM ME AS YOU READ THIS BOOK.

I'm here to be your coach and cheerleader. For me, it's all about appreciation and contribution. I don't want to give back in a little way, but in a massive way.

I've made plenty of mistakes in my life as a hairdresser and business owner, and I'll tell you what I would have done differently — you know, so you don't make them too.

I want to help accelerate your learning and your success. One of the ultimate joys of my job is watching a student advance in their skills and knowledge. It feels amazing to see learning and understanding in action; to see a student's body language and facial expression change as their confidence builds. And it just builds from there because my excitement ignites their passion and energy.

I promise to share with you the lessons I've learned over the past thirty years. I've made plenty of mistakes in my life as a hairdresser and business owner, and I'll tell you what I would have done differently — you know, so you don't make them too. Like the time I cut a client's hair way too short. Or the time I started a woman's hair, couldn't finish and had to call my boss over to finish the job. I've learned how to do things right. Of course, everyone makes mistakes, but many of them can be avoided.

This book highlights my Top 10 tips which will guide you to becoming fully booked. Some are technical, some are about how you act on the job and in life — but I've found that they all work. And when you practice them all together all the time, you really will be Booked Solid and make that a habit:

1. Be on time.
2. Dress in a way that tastefully honors our profession.
3. Be prepared.
4. Greet the client with enthusiasm.
5. Ask what I call the 'Knock Out Questions'.
6. Keep learning.
7. Manage your time.
8. Use your resources.
9. Surround yourself with great people.
10. Love what you do!

We'll be exploring these 10 concepts in depth throughout the book.

Finally, in case you didn't know, I like to have fun. Being a hairdresser is fun — and so is the process of becoming fully booked. You can dress in a creative way, put good music on in the salon, have a great time talking to your clients and continually improve and reach for excellence as a stylist. Find the salon that fits your unique style. Most importantly, have a terrific attitude.

Do you know what I've discovered? Most people tend to focus on what they *don't* have. "I don't have enough clients, don't make enough money, I don't have the life I want."

I'm going to encourage you to think in a new way. Instead of thinking about what you don't have, think about what you already have, and about what you want to have. Be grateful for what you've got or dream big dreams aimed toward what you want. The ultimate outcome in life is to…EXPAND Your Happiness. It can only bring you great success.

HERE'S WHAT I EXPECT FROM YOU AS YOU READ THIS BOOK.

I want you to read the whole book — even if you take bite sized pieces. Each chapter, each tip, each story of success or failure — they will all help you to become booked solid. When you're done, I want you to walk away with a wealth of information and the knowledge that you have a trusted resource in your library!

Whenever you're feeling stuck, pick the book up again — start anywhere — and my wish is that you will find helpful and supportive words, not to mention inspiration to get you back on track to becoming booked solid. If this book helps you, I hope you'll share it with others — someone looking for a change of career, one of your fellow hairdressers that could use a boost and more clients. The more people who succeed the better.

My biggest expectation is that you will read this book and then take action. I want you to work hard. Soak up information like a strand of hair painted with this season's blonde. I believe that if you follow the guidance of my book, you will be a success. You'll feel outstanding, you'll feel proud of your accomplishments and you'll be booked solid for life!

I don't want you to give up on this book. Do you know that the average person that buys a book never gets past the first chapter? Don't be one of those people. Go for it. It will be hard, but if you're serious about taking it to the next level in becoming booked solid, you will read right through this book again and again and again, until it sticks and becomes part of your language and part of your life.

TOP 10 TIPS

1 Be on time. In fact, be early. I recommend that you arrive 15 minutes before your first client. Not only is it your job to be ready and waiting, but if you get a late start in the morning, you're likely to mess up your schedule for the entire day. Your clients are busy and they expect to get their cut and color when their appointment card says they will! Really, it's a sign of respect — for the client's time and their patronage. Just think how it makes you feel when clients show up late to their appointments. Do unto others as you'd have them do to you!

2 Dress in a way that tastefully exemplifies our profession and, at the same time, shows off your artistic creativity. Have fun and be unique in your wardrobe expression. Make sure that you feel good in what you're wearing and about what you're wearing. It's also important to be comfortable. Don't wear shoes that look good but that will feel terrible when you'll be standing all day. When actresses get ready to appear on a talk show, they do the "chair test". They sit in a chair and make sure that the dress falls okay, that it doesn't ride up too much and that nothing is showing that they don't want shown. When hairdressers get dressed, we need to do our own version of the "chair test". Get dressed and go through all of the bending, twisting and leaning movements that you go through as you shampoo, cut and color someone's hair. Make sure that your outfit works.

3 Be prepared. Don't just be there. Take the time to look at the appointment book and find out what client it is and what they're coming in for. Then get the implements and tools you'll need for them, and set-up for color or other chemical services. Make sure your station is clean and inviting.

4 Greet the client with enthusiasm. Do you know the most important word in the English language? It's your client's first name. Use it and start your time with your client by making them feel known, good, and important. This is their time.

5 Ask the "Knock Out Questions" during your consultation with your client:
A. Do you prefer your hair long, mid-length or short?
B. Do you wear your hair on your face or off your face?
C. Do you use a blowdryer, a curling iron, or a flat iron?
D. How much time to do you spend on your hair every day?
E. Are there any specific products that you like to use?
F. What kind of work do you do; what's your lifestyle like?

6 Keep learning and continue your education. This is critical. Not only will it keep you booked because you'll know the latest cuts, trends, colors, and products, but ongoing education will keep you inspired and fresh. We will never know it all. After thirty years in the business, I'm still learning, and I'm still hungry to know what's next and to be on the cutting edge. In the fashion industry, trends are always changing and we have to keep our finger on the pulse.

7 Manage your time. There are many factors at play here. You want to be fully booked, but you also need to make sure that you can make all of your appointments, that you don't get tired or burned out, and that you make time for family, friends, other interests and, most importantly, yourself. If you do these things, you will be happy and feel fulfilled and those positive feelings will spill over onto your clients. I've used many tools for time management including calendars, schedules and setting clear boundaries with the booking receptionist at my salons.

8 Use your resources. Most of us think we have to make it all on our own. But while you are expected to pull your own weight, be professional, and act responsibly, you don't have to do it all alone. When you have a question, need support, or just need someone to listen, it's important to talk to someone that you trust who has your best interests at heart. This may be a mentor, teacher, or colleague. And don't worry about taking up their time because soon enough someone will surely come looking for your help. Resources also come in the form of style magazines, books like this one, conferences and trade shows. They all provide inspiration and helpful information.

9 Surround yourself with great coaches and great people. Have you ever heard the expression, "If you lay down with dogs, you're going to come up with fleas?" Well, this is what they mean. With hairdressing and with life, I encourage you to surround yourself with good people, no, *outstanding* people. Find the people who make you feel good, support you, and want you to grow. Luckily many people in our industry fit the bill. Find the right fit for you.

10 Love what you do...and you'll never work a day in your life. That's the truth. Get inspired and have a great attitude. Your clients will love to be around you, they'll look forward to it and they'll want you to cut their hair forever (and they'll tell all of their friends). When you are positive and joyful, when you take pride in your work, then you will surely be booked solid. Let's create that raving fan and not just a satisfied customer. One way to do that is to continuously do beautiful hair!

CHAPTER 2

My Story

"If you're coasting, you must be going downhill." — Joe Albertson

I want you to have big dreams, but don't walk out of your house and try to reach the moon on the first step. Have a plan, be methodical... you'll get there.

When I look back on my life and my journey to where I am now — the owner of the successful DiGrigoli Salon and School of Cosmetology and a national motivational and business speaker — I can tell you something for certain: what kept me alive and moving uphill was a combination of determination, persistence, perseverance and GUTS.

Why? Because we all make mistakes, that's how we learn, improve and grow. I've been fortunate enough that seeing my weaknesses, recognizing them, and then changing my behaviors has made all the difference. I really didn't have any mentors growing up as a child, or even when I went to cosmetology school. I think today it is extremely important to be surrounded by good mentors and people who walk the talk. And believe me; I think that's what we're missing today — good mentors, good leadership, and good role models. We are drowning in technology, but starving for guidance.

One thing I've learned about myself was that when I took action without thinking, it never turned out well and usually hurt me. You see, I could always visualize exactly what I wanted in my mind — I had my eyes on the prize. But, in my younger years, I was too ambitious and too excited. I bit off more than I could chew. My mind and my ideas wanted more than my back could carry.

As soon as I figured this out, I learned how to make a plan. I'm not saying you shouldn't have big dreams. I want you to have big dreams, but don't walk out of your house and try to reach the moon on the first step. Have a plan, be methodical...you'll get there. Here's how I did it...pitfalls, surprises, mistakes, and ultimate success.

HIGH SCHOOL

I really wasn't a good student in high school. The thing that got me through was sports. It wasn't that I didn't want to be a good student, but, honestly, I didn't have the tools. My parents never asked me for my report card, and I didn't receive the message that my education was important. My parents weren't interested, so neither was I. I was really good at sports, but didn't get a scholarship because I didn't even know what one was. No one explained that to me. When I was in high school my guidance counselor said that I should be a truck driver.

As for my schoolwork, I had to read things twice, three times to understand them. To me, learning wasn't fun. In fact, it was painful. I only wanted to focus on the things I was interested in — business yes, history no.

Now I know that the more you pay attention to people, the more their productivity increases.

At the time, I didn't understand, but I was living one of the main principles of this book. **If you do what you love, you'll never work a day in your life.** When it was time for algebra and social studies, it felt bad. But, when I was playing sports or learning about business, it was easy, it felt good. I was naturally drawn to the subjects and activities that felt good and were joyful, and it was there that I found my focus.

BERKSHIRE COMMUNITY COLLEGE

When I finished high school, I entered Berkshire Community College. Because I had missed so much in the years before, I had to go to my aunt (the English teacher) for help with my literature courses. All of that pain and struggle drove me because I knew what I *didn't* want. And I was determined to move towards what I *did* want. I had to learn how to learn, which I think is so important to students today. They have to learn <u>how</u> to learn, especially hairdressers. You either <u>have</u> to do something or you <u>want</u> to do something. When you *want* to do it, you have built in motivation. When you *have* to do something, it kind of takes away your passion.

I lasted for six months and then I quit. I couldn't stand being stuck at a desk listening to a teacher, or confined to a cubicle in the library. I'm a people person and I love people. I love finding out who they are, what they do, what they're interested in — everything! I knew that I had to get out and socialize. I needed to find a place where I could work with people.

COSMETOLOGY SCHOOL

I come from a long line of hairdressers, including my grandfather, my uncle, my aunts, and my dad and for some reason my grandfather wanted everyone to be a barber or a hairdresser. Then again my parents strongly discouraged me from going down that road and following in their footsteps. They told me that all I'd get were varicose veins and hemorrhoids, certainly no money.

I always used to cut my friends' hair at my dad's barber shop, it was just one of those things I could just do. My uncle, who was successful as a barber, was the only one who gave me encouraging advice. He told me to go to the big city for 5–10 years. He said, "When you come back, you'll be a superstar." So, I left my small town and headed out on my own.

On the way to the "big" city of Boston, I stopped in the medium-sized city of Springfield, Massachusetts where I enrolled at Springfield Technical Community College (STCC) for cosmetology school.

I didn't have a lot of money when I got there, maybe $500 in the bank, and I lived at the YMCA in a 300 square foot apartment on the 3rd floor. My bed was on cinderblocks so that I could store things underneath — the room was so small, there was nowhere else to put my stuff! I washed my dishes in the bathtub and my "kitchen" consisted of a mini-fridge from a yard sale and a toaster oven. I drove an old green Volkswagen I bought for $100. It worked pretty well, if you ignored the fact that it didn't have reverse gear. One time, the battery, which was located in the backseat, fell out on the highway.

FIRST JOB, FIRST COURSE, FIRST PLAN

Before my first semester in cosmetology school was complete, I had my first job at Lords and Ladies Salon at the local Holyoke Mall. I started learning as much as I could, and I also started saving. Soon enough, I had enough money to attend my first hair cutting course. It was at Vidal Sassoon in Santa Monica, California. It's amazing that now all of a sudden I became totally addicted to education and training.

I was in the airport after completing that week-long course, perusing a magazine at the candy shop, when I noticed this magazine called Success. I randomly opened it up to an article about goal setting by Ken Blanchard. I read it, I went to my briefcase and I pulled out an old envelope. On the back, I began to write my 25 year plan.

ON THE ROAD TO BECOMING BOOKED SOLID

When I got back home to the YMCA, I put my plan into action. Every night, I would spend an hour in the lobby recruiting people to cut their hair. I went to the beauty store outlets to buy products; I'd mark them up and sell them to my lobby clients. Word got around at the Y pretty fast that I was cutting hair, and I got busy fast. I charged three dollars a cut. And I practiced — my hairdressing techniques and my hairdresser/client techniques. I took initiative and found opportunity, money and experience — I pulled it out of thin air.

Before I go on with the story, I have to tell you this, because I'll never forget it. Three years ago, I was in my office and the receptionist called me over the intercom. She said, "Paul, there's a lady out here that wants to speak to you." I walked into the salon, and this woman says, "Paul do you remember me? You gave me the best perm I've ever had in my life in your tiny room at the Y." She had followed me over time and had come into the salon for an appointment. We shared a great laugh and it was exciting for us both to see how far I'd come from that little room! I thought back to say wow, I used to live in a 300 square foot apartment doing hair (my bathroom is bigger than that now) to standing in my salon that is 5,000 square feet. It kind of took me by surprise. It amazes me because I'm standing in my building now which is 10,000 square feet. So my point is clear, don't lose your vision, stay strong and extremely focused.

During cosmetology school and after graduation, I used to go to as many continuing education programs as I could. I was always asking questions, always offering to help. Hair shows were a great place to get experience, learn, and make contacts. My plan was to go into the back room and let the distributors know that I wanted to assist the guest hairdressers if they needed me. They almost always did. I'd wash out colors, rinse perms, shampoo for the guest artist, sweep the floors — anything they needed. And I always felt like I was learning more than I would have just sitting in the audience.

A NEW PARTNER

At one of these shows, I met a woman named Donna. She was always helping and in the thick of things. She kind of took a liking to me because of my energy, passion and knowledge and because I was fast and helpful. I could tell she was smart and driven to succeed, so I would do what she asked immediately.

After that show, I got a phone call from Donna. She asked me if I wanted to come work for her salon, a successful three-chair operation. But that wasn't really where I wanted to go, it was too small. So I said no and told her I already had a job. So what did she do? She called me again, and said, "Just come check it out." I thought it was the wrong thing to do, it wasn't what my plan called for. Still, I really liked her, she was a great person. So I went to meet her.

The salon was great and Donna wanted to put me on the floor right away. I didn't think I was ready, but I took the job and worked at both salons, New York New York Hair Salon and Lords & Ladies. After graduating from STCC, I left Lords and Ladies and decided to work with her full time for New York New York Hair Salon.

We got along so well, but after about a year and a half, I started thinking about moving on to a bigger salon. As I was thinking it over Donna took over the business from the former owner. She saw my drive, my passion and my VISION. So she asked me to become her partner.

What an incredible run we had. We worked together for ten years, and in that time we grew from one salon to two and then built an incredible team of hairdressers. We had flexibility and freedom, frequently arranging our schedules so that we could play ping pong in the middle of day over our lunch break. As our success grew, so did our relationship — we were ideal business partners and great friends. Because we were on the same path, we never fought, we never even disagreed for an entire decade.

But, like they say, change is inevitable. Eventually, our personal lives changed, our priorities went in different directions and we parted ways.

OUT ON MY OWN

My priority at that point was to become a national spokesman for the hair industry, I wanted to own five salons (I had three at that point), to open a cosmetology school for beginners, and to run an advanced academy for hairdressers to continue their education. I ended up with everything but the five salons.

One of my best friends, Tommy Goodrow, previously VP of Economic Development at STCC, introduced me to Steve Spunelli. Steve had once owned 35 Jiffy Lube auto service centers and after selling every last one, was teaching at Babson College in the Entrepreneurial Department. He told me that his 40 MBA students did a case study on an existing franchise every year. I asked him if they ever did their study on a non-existing franchise, because I was thinking about going down that road. He said, no, but that it was an interesting proposition. He went off to ask his students if they'd be willing to do a viability study to find out if franchising was right for DiGrigoli Salons. They were!

It was a fantastic experience. They looked at everything and dissected it. In the end, they decided that franchising was not the best path for me at that time, and they had some very interesting questions to ask me. There was one that I couldn't answer.

They asked, "Do you feel the client is loyal to the brand or to the stylist?"

At that time, most of my people had been with me for 14–15 years (which by the way, was unheard of in the industry). I had no idea what happened when stylists left...but I was going to find out.

Five years after the case study, my salons were chosen to be among the "Super 60" by the Springfield Chamber of Commerce. This was a huge deal as it celebrated the 60 fastest growing, local, small businesses in the area. Things were going incredibly well, until the local news took notice. A newspaper article featured the Super 60 and clearly stated that one of the qualifications was that your revenue had to exceed one million dollars. We made 1.3 million dollars that year.

Two of my hairdressers read the article and jumped to the conclusion that I was a millionaire. They didn't understand what it takes to pay fourteen stylists and staff, the mortgage on three buildings, insurance, taxes and more.

They left and took five other stylists with them to start their own salon. Overnight, I lost 49% of my clientele and revenue. But, I did find out the answer to the MBA students' question. Of the 49% we lost initially, 21% came back after six months. The reasons they gave for leaving the new salon were:
- Clients weren't getting calls back,
- Customer service changed for the worse,
- Availability decreased because time management decreased,
- Parking and location were not convenient, and
- Answering machine, no receptionist.

REBUILDING

When the seven stylists left, I got a huge wake-up call and I almost lost everything.

To survive, I downsized by selling two of my three salons. Now I just had the school, one salon, and my speaking engagements. What started out as a huge catastrophe actually brought me back to life and turned into a windfall. I got distracted by my plans for expansion, but when I got my focus back, I pulled all my work into arm's reach again. The salon and the school were in the same building. The school allowed me to build relationships with my students and pull them over to work in the salon (once licensed) if it felt right. Everything was great again. What a learning experience! You won't find this information in a textbook. Believe me, if owning your own salon was easy, everyone would be doing it.

How did I get my focus back? Pain and resilience. You don't move until you get enough pain to move you. I got distracted because there was so much to do, everyone needed attention and I wasn't there enough. There wasn't enough of me to go around, I could never do enough. Maybe in your life the expansion isn't three salons, maybe it's something else. But you know it's too much when you get distracted and it starts to fall apart.

As I refocused, I became stronger mentally, physically, emotionally and financially. I became a better person, my leadership changed, I improved my communication skills. When seven people leave, you have to reevaluate. I turned the negative into a positive.

It's almost we needed to hit rock bottom in order to grow like crazy. Once again, I was booked solid...now let's get you there too.

CHAPTER 3

Why Be a Hairdresser?

Being a hairdresser is in my blood, but once I got going in school (and in the lobby at the YMCA), it wasn't long before I realized what a great profession it is. So, even if I fell into it because of my family, it was absolutely the right choice for me. It's about people and being social; it's never boring; there is no glass ceiling — the ability to grow and flourish is astounding; and, it just feels good.

The possibilities are endless. Just follow the need for beauty.

YOU ENJOY PEOPLE

If you enjoy people and like to talk, if you love learning about people — listening to them and sharing yourself with them- then this job is definitely for you. You have to be a people person to be a hairdresser. First, you have to be able to communicate with your clients to find what they want done with their hair. If you can't really listen — then you'll never be fully booked.

Do you know why?

When a busy mom mentions her children, soccer practice, the PTA, and her book club, some red flags should go up in your head. Would you give her a complicated haircut that demands a lot of work on her part every morning before going out in public? No way. You want to give this mom a stunning cut that looks like she spent an hour and a million bucks, when, in fact, it took her about 5 minutes and the cost of a great haircut and a few styling products.

It's incredibly important that you talk to your clients, ask them the right questions and really listen to and respect their answers. This is the **first step** towards becoming booked solid with the client. People, in general, want to be seen, heard and respected. When you can give them that simple gift while they're sitting in your chair, they're going to want to stay there.

You'll need to pay attention when a client regales you with stories of a chemical sensitivity — you won't want to give her a perm. Make sure to hear when a teenager tells you that she had her hair cut short once before and it was a disaster — and leave her hair long!

The **second step** is about building the relationship. The more you get to know your client, the stronger the relationship will be. Learn about their interests, their work, their hobbies, their families. And the more you learn about them, the more insight you'll have into their look and style, and what their beauty needs are. And let them learn about you. Let them know you enough to be pleased to see you — not only because their hair will look outstanding when they leave, but also because they enjoy sitting in your chair and talking to you. So make them your friend. Friends buy from friends.

Have you ever been to a hairdresser that didn't talk? It's not fun. When it happened to me, I felt like I was intruding, like the stylist didn't like me and she couldn't wait for me to leave. As a result, I couldn't wait to leave, and I didn't want to go back.

Make your chair a fun place, a warm place, and a place that people look forward to sitting in — again and again and again.

YOU ARE CREATIVE AND ARTISTIC

Every time a client sits in your chair, you have a challenge. You need to give them what they want and you need to come up with a cut and style that suits who they are. But you also need to put your own flair in there. Because you're creative, because you're artistic, view your client's hair as a sculpture waiting for your personal touch.

You get to play with color, texture and length. You get to pick your genre: classic, modern, retro, punk, urban, youthful or mature. You get to be on the cutting edge of style. You have the ability to start your own trends.

Beyond the creativity and artistry that you offer your clients, being a hairdresser is not a uniformed gig. With the way that you dress and do your own hair, you get to express your style, and your art as well. It's an opportunity. Use your own self as a canvas to attract clients to your salon and into your chair. Set an example of how anyone can use themselves to express who they are — inspire your clients to do the same.

YOU CAN MAKE EXCELLENT MONEY

First of all, you will make money as a hairdresser every single day because of tips. Obviously, the more solidly you keep your chair booked, the more tips and wages you will make. There's really no cap on your wages, because it is up to you to decide how many services you offer, how much you want to work and, frankly, how good you want to get. We are in control of our own destiny. We all have the same 24 hours, what you do with them is up to you. That's for sure.

Think about that. You get to decide what learning opportunities you want to take, how much education you want to get, how often you receive advanced training — and *your* decisions influence your ultimate success. If you're good, you can work in any area. But you can make money and be successful, If you're outstanding.

The number of services you offer is critical. If you only cut hair, your chances of becoming fully booked decreases. For example, let's say 50 people come into the salon every day. If they want a haircut, they have 10 stylists to choose from — because you all cut hair — so your chances of being chosen are one in 10. But if they also want color, they have fewer stylists to choose from because maybe only five of the stylists do color. So now your chances are one in five. Add another service, and your odds get even better. Stand out with your knowledge, expertise and experience. Stay booked solid because you can truly take care of whatever your clients need.

The more valuable you become to the marketplace, the more money you make. Most of all, be known as an expert in your chosen field, whether it's color, men and women's haircuts, updos, waxing. Because today women that are 70 want to look 60, women who are 60 want to look 50, women that are 50 want to look 40, and that applies to the male market as well. Think about it, consumers spend 60.5 billion dollars each year on just hair care and cosmetics alone. Women spend 12.5 billion dollars on color alone. I said this before, and I think it's worth saying again: no matter how big the information age gets, no one will ever take our job. You're never going to walk down the street and have someone ask you, "Did you get your hair cut on the Internet?"

The more valuable you become to the marketplace, the more money you will make.

YOUR GROWTH POTENTIAL IS UNLIMITED

Beyond services you can offer as a hairdresser, you can grow in this profession in other ways as well. Within the salon itself, you can grow from being an assistant, to a junior hairdresser, to a senior hairdresser, to a salon manager and to an owner. In my salon, there are five levels you can progress through. This will differ from one salon to another.

There are also growth options outside of the salon. With your experience — the experience that can grow and grow — you can specialize in styling for photo shoots, TV, movies and theater. You can do hair on a cruise ship, be a platform artist, become an art director, or work on the runways. As I speak across the country and talk to many top stylists, most of them tell me that they do not take new clients. I feel when you do that you're shooting yourself in the foot because you have two opportunities here. You're adapting to a new client, and you can raise your prices. So ALWAYS take new clients.

The possibilities are endless. Just follow the need for beauty.

YOU MAKE PEOPLE FEEL OUTSTANDING

I've already talked about how important it is to serve your clients to keep them coming back, and to keep the job feeling good for yourself. This is a major theme of this book. If this is part of who you are, if you love to be around people and make them feel good, then you are set for life as a hairdresser. You need to know it's not about you. It's always client first. Listen to the client, ask penetrating questions, and do whatever you can to make them feel fabulous. You make people feel outstanding. You're not selling a haircut or a color, you're selling a feeling. You're selling emotion.

EVERY DAY IS DIFFERENT

If you crave repetition, boredom and the same old, same old, then being a hairdresser is not for you. You aren't working in a factory when you step through the doors of a salon. Every client brings their unique personality, needs, wants and hair to the chair. As each person sits down, you get the chance to have fresh eyes and a new start. The days move fast as you move from new experience to new experience.

Of course, as you become fully booked, you'll have the joy of seeing many of your clients on a regular basis — maybe every 4-8 weeks, depending on their needs. But even when you see them, there won't be repetition — their hair will change with their lives or with the seasons. Their needs and wants for styling will change as they get new jobs, have kids, find new boyfriends. And your challenge will be to change with them — and greet the change with open arms.

YOU ARE MOTIVATED BY YOUR WORK AND FUN

Bottom line, hairdressing is a fun, social, exciting career. It's a great way to spend your days and your life. Keep it fun, crazy, playful, outrageous, but also keep it professional. When I talk internationally, many people who attend my seminars say to me, "Paul you can truly motivate anyone." And I say, "That might be true, but what if that person's an idiot and you motivate them? Then all you have is a motivated idiot."

Amanda

I WENT TO COLLEGE FOR FOUR YEARS, BUT I KNEW WHAT I always wanted to do: hair. I had recommended the DiGrigoli School of Cosmetology to a friend and I went to visit her at the school after graduation. At that moment, I knew where I was meant to be. I knew I'd regret it for the rest of my life if I didn't go after my dream.

It took me 9 months to complete my courses at the School of Cosmetology. I was "head of the class", according to Paul. I had a plan. In order to avoid student loans and to reach my goal of being a hairdresser as soon as possible, I went to school every day from 9am to 4pm, then went to work at a restaurant from 5pm to close where I was a waitress and a bartender. When I got home, I studied, slept, and started it all over again the next morning. I was in turbo mode.

Part of my success, beyond **my hard work,** is that I've **taken every** opportunity to **learn what I can.**

My focus was strong and it paid off. As soon as I graduated from the School of Cosmetology and got my license, I started working for Paul at the DiGrigoli Salon. But I kept my restaurant job until I had built a solid clientele and felt stable enough to make hairdressing my full-time job. Luckily, my co-workers and I already had a nice clientele at the restaurant — and we handed out my new hairdressing business cards to our customers. The restaurant business also lends itself to good old fashioned networking. It's a perfect place for casual conversations like, "I love your hair!" or "Are you in school?" All easy lead-ins for me to tell them what I was really up to and make a connection.

Before long, I was ready to leave the restaurant. I began as a Junior stylist and moved up quickly to a Senior stylist position. Soon after, Paul asked me to take on the Salon Coordinator position as well, purchasing products, scheduling the salon, and planning fun community events like the annual hair show at Mass Mutual and the local St. Patrick's Day parade. I didn't think that being a hairdresser would involve building parade floats, but at DiGrigoli it does and we have a blast. It's been two years since graduation, and I've been promoted again to Master Stylist and Salon Manager.

Part of my success, beyond my hard work, is that I've taken every opportunity to learn what I can. I go to every show with Paul, I take on new challenges. I've seen firsthand that the more you put into this work and this life, the more you get out of it.

Paul always tells us to surround ourselves with positive and passionate people. I took his advice and I enjoy working with him everyday. Everyone in the salon shares his spirit — it's contagious, so it's impossible not to! As a boss and a mentor, he gives us freedom, never micromanaging, but always there to guide and support. This is because we've built a relationship of trust, but more importantly, it's because Paul wants everyone around him to succeed. He wants us to learn from his mistakes and his successes and do everything he's done — but faster, stronger, and better.

I appreciate that I've been given the opportunity to learn more than just hair, I've also learned the business side of things which is something I didn't expect. This has been a great experience — because of my hard work and because of the passionate, kind and supportive people that I work with at the Salon. I really couldn't ask for anything more. Though I have a feeling things are just going to keep getting better and better!

CHAPTER 4

Clients: Without 'Em, You're Just a Person With Scissors

If you want to become Booked Solid, you have to create raving fans. You have to generate the "WOW" factor. If the client leaves thinking, "I just got a haircut," then you haven't quite accomplished your mission. They should leave saying, "Wow!" Your goal is to make them feel outstanding. Not just good.

When something is outstanding, it stands out. Your clients should get compliments. Their friends and even strangers will want to know who cut their hair. As a hairdresser, I would keep cutting your hair the same way — until you told me that the compliments had stopped, and you stopped having that "WOW" feeling. You have to remember that every client leaves your salon with your autograph on their head.

Client retention is critical to being Booked Solid. You need the steady business of returning clients and you need the

When you are highly trained as a hairdresser, stylist, colorist and more, you are offering convenience and one stop shopping to your clients.

35

CLIENT RETENTION
Four reasons clients
LEAVE
▶ Poor technical
   skills
▶ Poor communica-
   tion
▶ Not professional
▶ Not understand-
   ing wants/needs

word of mouth that they spread to bring in a never ending stream of new clients. As you go through your days behind the chair, some clients will stay and some will go. If you understand why, you can actually do something about it. If you recognize the reasons that they're leaving, you can make changes to your work to help them stay. It's up to you.

FOUR REASONS CLIENTS LEAVE

1. Poor technical skills. Even though I believe that 85% of your success depends on your attitude and only 15% relies on your technical abilities, that 15% is critical. If you don't have confidence, experience and skill with the actual techniques of cutting, color, and styling, your clients will leave. The solution is practice, education, and training. Practice makes perfect. However, when you do practice, make it a perfect practice.

2. Poor communication. When it comes to their hair and their look, clients need engagement. They need to feel like they can tell you anything and that you will really listen to them. You must engage with them, ask the right questions, listen to their words and their needs. For example, if the goal is to texturize the hair and remove the bulk, and a client says, "Paul, it's too puffy on the top." Great, easy, I can fix that without a problem. If you don't open clear lines of communication, the client can't get what they need and they'll leave. They'll find someone who can hear them and help them.

3. Unprofessional. Your client's experience should be positive. If you show up late and unprepared, you're wasting their time. If you're not dressed appropriately and you're chewing gum in their ear, it shows bad taste. And if you don't listen and you have a negative attitude, you're turning them off. The end result will be that you've ruined the trust relationship. The client won't feel safe or good in your chair. If you're running behind it creates stress, and stress will not allow you to do your best work.

4. Self-centered. If you haven't figured it out yet, the road to being Booked Solid is by treating your clients like royalty. Listening, understanding, asking the right questions. The appointment isn't about you. Your client has come to your chair to be pampered. Not understanding or, worse, not paying attention to their wants and needs will likely send them running from your chair.

FOUR REASONS CLIENTS <u>STAY</u>

1. Consistency. You will be Booked Solid because you will deliver for your clients every time. They know what to expect — great service and a great haircut — every time they sit in your chair. You're always professional, you always do exactly what they want, you always exceed their expectations. Here's the big question, who cuts your hair and why?

2. Great attitude. Do you like hanging out with miserable people? Be likeable and positive in every way with your client — about their hair and their look, but also about their life. As you get to know your clients, you have the opportunity to be helpful and over deliver in every way. For instance, if they mention

CLIENT RETENTION
Four reasons clients STAY
▶ Consistency
▶ Great attitude/likeable
▶ Education level
▶ Availability

they need a new car, mention that your brother works at the dealer across town. If they need childcare, maybe one of your friends runs a home daycare. When you really listen, you'll hear ways that you can contribute. Bottom line: make your chair a happy place. Never hang around someone who's a wet blanket.

3. Education & service level. Clients will stay with you if you can offer them everything they need from your chair. This is about convenience as much as anything else. Once upon a time, when people went shopping, they had to go to the butcher for meat, the grocer for produce, the baker for bread and on and on. They had to visit several stores for all of the items on their list. Today we have supermarkets, and one-stop shopping is a major modern convenience. You'll hear ads boasting that "it's all under one roof."

When you are highly trained as a hairdresser, stylist, colorist and more, you are offering convenience and one stop shopping to your clients. Why would they stay with you for a cut when they have to go somewhere else for color — when that colorist could also give them a great haircut? The more you know and the more you can do, the better.

4. *Availability.* After you read this book and put these techniques into practice, you will be Booked Solid. So, how can

you still stay available for your clients? Planning is everything. At the end of each service, tell your client how long the cut or color will last and when they should return. You can even walk with them to the reception desk and let the receptionist know the date as well. This way, the client won't be faced with calling you for an appointment when they need you immediately and find that you're booked — forcing them into someone else's chair or another salon.

Another great offering is to work the hours that your clients need. Perhaps you could add a couple of late nights or an early morning. Ask your clients what they need or just open up at different times and find out what works. When you accommodate them, they are appreciative and want to stay in your chair, the place where all of their needs are met.

CHAPTER 5

Evaluate Yourself

Whether you're just starting out and mapping your work as a hairdresser or you're already in the game, it's important that you take stock of what you have, what you want, and how you'll get from point A to point B. This includes taking a close look at your clientele, ways to improve your business methods, while also making sure you're an incredible service provider.

You want to look forward to going in to work every day, because if you dread it, your clients will notice.

DO YOU KNOW WHO YOUR CLIENTELE IS?

Think about it, if your clientele is 70 year-olds in Miami, you need to train to take care of their specific hair needs. If your clientele operates in the fashion world, you need to learn weaves and color. You need to know what your clients will want and become an expert in that arena. In

DO YOU KNOW YOUR CLIENTELE?

▶ Age group
▶ Male/female
▶ Chemical services
▶ Esthetic services
▶ Manicures/ pedicures

effect, you are finding your niche and you can be known as *the* hairdresser that does fabulous up-dos, proms and formals or urban colors. Whatever it is that your client base wants.

When evaluating your client group, take into account their:
- Age group
- Gender
- Culture
- Lifestyle

Do they need:
- Esthetic services (facials, eyebrows, facial waxing, make-up)
- Manicures/pedicures
- Color/foils & partial foils
- Perms/waves/relaxers
- Weaves/Up-dos

HOW CAN YOU IMPROVE?

Manage your time. Time management is critical for a successful business. When you're in the salon, schedule your appointments correctly so that you don't keep clients waiting. Know how long it takes to do a foil, a perm, a complete makeover. Make sure that you schedule personal breaks in between so that you can eat and take care of yourself and not get grumpy with clients.

Outside of the salon, you also need to place a high premium on personal time.

Do things other than hairdressing; enjoy your friends, families and hobbies. The most important thing here is that you don't get burned out. You want to look forward to going in to work every day, because if you dread it, your clients will notice. Also, master the important skill of learning to say 'no'. If someone wants you to take a client for them or fill in when they go out of town, make sure that it really fits into your schedule and makes sense for you. Don't be held hostage by your work. Live your life! Don't burn out, burn up.

Create positive habits. Repetition is the mother of skill. It's important that you practice the things that you want to stick over and over again. This includes your technical skills — all kinds of cuts, colors, esthetic services and beyond. But, it also includes your professional skills or behaviors. Showing up early, being prepared, engaging your clients, and taking care of them with class. The more you act the way you want to be, the easier it will get. Most important, be yourself.

Don't be lazy in learning. I encourage my students and the hairdressers that work in my salon to always seek out new skills through education, training and seminars. You need to stay on top of the latest trends and new advancements through magazines, TV, Internet, movies and fashion shows. You can even learn a lot through observation. As you meet more and more people in the field, you can learn from each other. It's not really how much money you make, it's what you will become.

Clarify your goals. Be crystal clear, because clarity is power. In terms of your business, how many hours do you want to work? How much money do you want to make? Do you want to be a master colorist? Or master esthetician? My philosophy is to have different kinds of goals-some that will be easy and fast, some that will be huge and long, perhaps a lifelong challenge.

My goal formula looks like this:

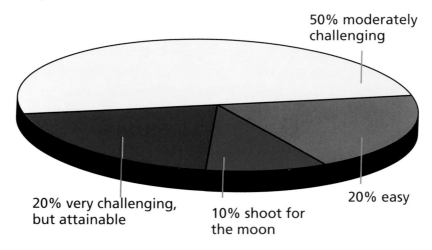

50% moderately challenging

20% very challenging, but attainable

10% shoot for the moon

20% easy

Let the easy goals and even the moderately challenging goals help build you up as you cross them off your list. Knowing that you are advancing and succeeding will only strengthen your ability and desire to reach those higher goals, which in return gives you great confidence.

EXECUTE THE SERVICE

Communicate clearly with clients. Always ask the right questions, clarify their requests and do exactly what they ask for. Remember it's their hair and they know best!

Develop your eye. This takes a bit of time, unless it comes naturally to you. Learn to understand the physicality of different people and how that affects which cuts and colors look good on them. This includes facial features — square, round, diamond, rectangular and oval faces; the type of hair — its quality, quantity, density, and texture; the coloring of the hair, the skin, the eyes, the mouth, even the clothes the client typically wears.

Understand balance. Unless it's the style, no one wants one side longer than the other. You also need to balance the hair to the face and to the body of the client. Also balance the hair against itself. For instance, very thin hair might not stand up, so to speak, in certain cuts meant to carry a lot of body. When you start to blow the hair dry, you'll get your best glimpse of how everything's balancing out. Take your time to make it right as you finish. I always say that if the cut looks good when it's wet, when you finish it; it becomes your bonus.

Pay attention to details. When a client sits in your chair, they're usually negative. They'll focus on what they see as their flaws. They'll point out their big nose, a mole on their neck, cowlicks and more. Your job is to focus on the positive, reassure them and make it better. You have the ability to minimize these perceived flaws with your styling abilities. Of course, listening to your clients' desires and needs is critical. In most cases, if you're a master at your craft, you will be able to turn your customer around making them feel outstanding within 30 minutes.

EXECUTE THE SERVICE
- ▶ Communicate clearly with clients
- ▶ Develop your eye
- ▶ Understand balance
- ▶ Pay attention to details

CHAPTER 6

How to Be a Poor Stylist

One of the most exciting things about our lives is that we're offered an infinite amount of choices. We can exercise or do nothing, go to school or not, read a book or watch TV, eat healthy food or go to a fast food restaurant. As a hairdresser, you will face many options — should you add another day to your schedule, learn to do color, travel to New York City for a new seminar...

But the most important choice you'll make is this: Do you want to be a poor stylist or an outstanding stylist? Being a poor stylist isn't as easy as it sounds, it's not just about being bad at cutting hair. I hope you'll choose to be outstanding...and just to be sure you can avoid them, I've outlined the steps to failure.

Do you want to be a poor stylist or an outstanding stylist? Being a poor stylist isn't as easy as it sounds, it's not just about being bad at cutting hair.

STEP 1. DON'T TAKE THE PROFESSION SERIOUSLY

This is easy enough, just treat hairdressing like a job instead of career. Don't plan for the future, don't make plans to grow through education. Just get up, go to work, cut some hair and go home. Hairdressing can just be your 9 to 5 and not your life if you treat it like something you "have" to do every day. Essentially, you'll just be going through the motions with no passion or discipline.

STEP 2. LACK FOCUS

Poor stylists are uncertain in all they do because they have no real purpose. Without focus, there are no goals, no vision, no motivation to change the way things are. This situation and mindset gets people stuck in what I call a "Figure Eight" pattern. It sends them around and around in loops with ups and downs, but they simply can't get off the track. And when you're stuck on the track, you can't grow or expand.

STEP 3. DON'T BE INTERESTED IN LEARNING MORE

There are actually three reasons why people take this step. First, sometimes they don't care enough about themselves or their futures to continue their education or training. Second, they don't believe in themselves enough to think they're worth the investment to learn more. They assume that what they know is equal to how far they are "supposed to" get in life. Finally, some people think they already know it all, their egos are way too big for their britches and so they see no reason to learn more. In fact, they believe there is nothing left to learn and that their skills are already perfect.

STEP 4. HAVE LOW EXPECTATIONS

If you think life is supposed to be mediocre, then it will be. If you think being a poor stylist is your lot in life, then it will be. These low expectations, of course, just continue to prove themselves correct and the stylist will make things very tough on his or her self. This usually involves a lot of complaining about life, work, the salon and the fact that they are going nowhere and that their chair is empty. That attitude will continue to chase clients away.

How to Be an Outstanding Stylist

This chapter is about the choice I hope you'll make. It outlines the steps you need to take to be an outstanding stylist. Let's go:

STEP 1. HAVE A SUPER ATTITUDE

Of course this is completely the opposite of the "poor stylist" route where the bad attitude pretty much rules every step towards mediocrity or failure. I encourage you to have fun and be positive — people will seek you out, hoping your happiness will be contagious. Things will go wrong, that's life — but it's up to you to make the right decision in dealing with it. For instance, don't whine and accept defeat, instead find the solution and go for it.

I always believe in resilience and having the ability to bounce back and put the stakes in the ground and go for it. It's

Every mistake you've made is a learning experience. Use it to your advantage because it certainly helps to drive you. It also helps you to hopefully make better decisions for the future.

51

HOW CAN YOU IMPROVE?

▶ Manage your time
▶ Make things a habit
▶ Don't be lazy in learning
▶ Clarify your goals

like any sport, when you get knocked down; you get back up again and get back in the game. It's not any different in the game of business. For example, if you cut someone's hair too short or you make a mistake with color, it's not the end of the world. You correct it and you get ready for your next client. Every mistake you've made is a learning experience. Use it to your advantage because it certainly helps to drive you. It also helps you to hopefully make better decisions for the future. I always say that we're in control of our own destiny. The salon owner can drive the customers through the door but once they're sitting in your chair, you have total control over whether or not they're going to continue coming back to you or they're going to leave you. If you're playing at the highest level and you are consistent on a daily basis, they will come back and without question you will become Booked Solid. So in other words, let disappointment drive you to be better. It's the recovery that gives us self confidence. Do your best not to take things personally.

Often times this means it's not the condition, but the decision that counts. Remember my story? I didn't just go to trade shows to watch, I dove in and put myself out there by volunteering to work and help out. As a result, I learned a tremendous amount and I made some incredible contacts. Most of all, I left quite an impression as someone who works hard and has a lot of passion.

Your super attitude needs you to be responsible. What this means is that you don't have a blame list. If you aren't Booked Solid, it's your responsibility and yours alone. These steps are right here for the taking and they work. If you think you aren't booked because of the location of your salon, then switch salons. Find a solution, take action and make it happen. If you don't have enough knowledge in color or cutting, maybe the salon that you're in isn't the right fit for you.

STEP 2. BE EXCITED ABOUT WHAT YOU DO

Have passion about our industry. This includes watching the latest trends, staying up to date and learning as much as you can. Hairdressing becomes not just a job, but also your hobby, a real interest of yours. When you have this passion, you can't help but to subscribe to as many trade magazines as possible, listen to CD's, subscribe to DVDs, and read great books from the industry. Excitement can lead you just about anywhere you want to go as you keep your eyes open and jump at the chance to learn more.

Burn out is not caused by working 12 hours a day. Burn out is caused by boredom and repetition; doing the same thing over and over again. In addition to that, I would highly recommend stop doing hair at home for your friends and your family and do them at the salon. I found that by doing hair for many years that if you burn the candle at both ends, you start to lose your passion and your energy for doing what you do best, and that's hair. I know some of you are thinking that it's a good way to make a little extra money and it helps to pay the bills and I think that's great. But when you become Booked Solid it's hard to do both and I think you'll agree with me. So at some point you have to learn how to say 'no' and ask your family and friends to come to the salon. This will help to eliminate burnout.

STEP 3. BEHAVE LIKE A PROFESSIONAL

When you act like a professional, you show people around you that you are a success, and that you have the capacity for even more. So, how do you do it? Here are a few tips:

- Arrive to work 15 minutes early
- Be prepared for your clients *before* they arrive
- Keep your space immaculate
- Look immaculate
- Dress the part, let your sense of style and creativity shine through tastefully in your choice of clothes, accessories, makeup and hair; develop your own personal image
- Always be courteous and nice
- Offer to help others when you can
- Be an asset to the salon with all of the above — inside and outside of work

STEP 4. BE A TEAM PLAYER

If you're already on your way with Steps 1 through 3, this one will be quite easy. To be a team player, you have to see that the whole salon suffers when any of the hairdressers act like "poor stylists." Imagine that you are busy doing a fantastic job in your own chair, delivering fantastic cuts and premium service to your clients but the guy next to you:

- Looks like a slob
- Bad attitude
- Uses foul language
- Doesn't help clean the coffee bar even when he has a free moment
- Is always in a terrible mood
- Has hair on the floor and a messy station

The list could go on and on. The point is, in that scenario, the other guy makes you look bad. Even though it isn't your behavior, it reflects poorly on the salon and everything in it — and it negatively impacts your client's experience along with salon experience.

Now that you've thought about how that feels when someone else isn't a team player, you'll understand how important it is that you *are* always a team player. Don't be lazy, be willing to help others as often as you can, think of the salon — not just yourself. And, finally, appreciate your salon-mates. These are your colleagues and your partners, when you all work well together, the whole team benefits. When you have chemistry on a team, you can't be beat.

EXECUTE THE SERVICE
- ▶ Communicate clearly with clients
- ▶ Develop your eye
- ▶ Understanding balance
- ▶ Pay attention to details

STEP 5. LEAD BY EXAMPLE

I should say, "be a leader." Leaders don't have to be told what to do, we're self-starters. Our initiative fills our chairs because we learn about new styles or tricks of the trade and then we bring them to the salon. As a side note to Step 4, this includes helping out around the salon to make it outstanding as well. For example, make new coffee if you take the last cup. If you're in the back and notice that the conditioner is running out at the shampoo station, bring it out with you. And by all means, clean out the refrigerator! Remember the client sitting in your chair is the superstar, not the person standing behind the chair. It's really not that hard to shine in this way, make the connection.

This step also has to do with confidence. When you feel certain about your path as a hairdresser and your techniques, other people notice and they want to do it right, like you. That confidence translates as comfort, something and someone to trust in the eyes of your clients.

Show others that you are a goal setter. Prove it by taking the steps to achieve your goals and show that you treat hairdressing like a career, not just a job. When you know your purpose as a hairdresser and you have set a high goal, it will show in your performance and in everything you do — standing behind your chair and beyond. You will reek of excellence and accomplishment, which is a good thing.

One last thing about leading by example. If you haven't figured it out already, being a hairdresser isn't a solo gig. You have to work well with other stylists, managers, the head of the show, the top dog on the movie set, and, of course, the person sitting in your chair. What this means is that you have to set the tone of collaboration and compromise for everyone. You might think an up-do is the way to go, someone else might think long and big is more on target. The best thing you can do is be open to change, looking at all sides. When you have a "my way or the highway" attitude, you'll turn people off and they'll end up taking off. I learn a great deal from my staff in the salon and the school.

STEP 6. REMEMBER YOUR CLIENTS

Because they will remember you — mostly for two reasons! 1. If you're not good at what you do. 2. You aren't professional or the experience was just unpleasant, they won't forget. If you're not good at what you do, you aren't professional or the experience is just unpleasant, they won't forget. They'll take one (or all) of the following actions: tell people to stay away from you, complain to your boss, or just never come back. Any way you slice it, you lose. In this case, even bad press isn't good press. It's just reason #1 to always do your best. Make sure you're known as an expert in your chosen field within your area. People always ask who the experts are.

On the other end of the spectrum, if you're really good, your clients won't forget and they'll tell everyone that they know. Word of mouth is the most powerful way to become Booked Solid. When you wow your clients, go the extra mile and make them feel outstanding, they will tell everyone they know. When your haircuts make total strangers stop your clients on the street and demand to know who cut their hair, you know you're doing it right. Your autograph is on every head that walks out of the door, so you can imagine the advertising for you. It will be a maximum 4–6 weeks before they return for their next haircut or color. As you know, most of our business is through referrals. The moral of this story? Treat your clients like gold, and it will all come back to you.

STEP 7. BE A GREAT HAIRDRESSER, TECH-NICALLY SPEAKING

You know that I believe that attitude is incredibly important to your success, but even the best attitude won't make you outstanding if you can't cut hair. Or, for that matter, if you only cut hair. Hone your craft with education, training and practice, practice, practice. Stay up to date on the latest trends, styles, products and technologies to enhance your work. Most importantly, learn as many techniques as you can and learn them well. The more you offer your clients, the less reason that they'll have to go anywhere else.

There are so many outstanding educational companies out there, you should learn everything you possibly can from the very best. Then apply it to your own creativity and pick up several techniques that can simplify your work as a haircutter and as a colorist. After being in the industry for a quarter of a century, there's not too much I haven't seen. Everything that I've learned from the basics to the most progressive, always ties together.

STEP 8. PERFORM, PERFORM, PERFORM

Outstanding hairdressers are in the top 3% in the country for retail sales (18–25% over service sales). They do a minimum of $3,000 per week in services, depending on their location. The price of the service is dictated by your personality, how well you communicate, and your skill level as a hairdresser. The more you know, the more you become valuable to the marketplace and the more money you will make.

What this means is that they are Booked Solid *and* taking care of all the pieces — personal, professional and the future — so that they are at the top of their game. These stylists can handle time management, self-care, making clients feel amazing and a great variety of serves with high skill.
Interestingly, even with these high sales numbers, they don't *sell* to clients, they *educate* them. Imagine two scenarios:

You need a car, so you go to the used car lot and some slimy guy approaches you and basically tries to persuade you to buy the car that he thinks is best for you. He doesn't ask you about yourself or what your needs are, it's clear that he doesn't care — he just wants your money.

You need a car, so you to go to the dealer and a nice guy approaches you and asks you what you're looking for in a car, what your lifestyle is like, how much you'd like to spend and more. Then, he takes you from car to car, providing you with the pros and cons of each one — in direct relation to the information you gave him about yourself. He's full of information, clearly knows his stuff.

Who are you going to want to buy from? Choice #2 is obvious! Now translate it to hairdressing. You want to be the hairdresser that knows about hair, fashion and beauty. You want to listen to your client's needs and then educate them on the best cuts and the best beauty routines for their situation. This builds trust and the client comes to rely on you for help, guidance, and gorgeousness!

STEP 9. BE ADDICTED TO EDUCATION AND TRAINING

This is all about becoming better and better at what you do and about becoming more and more excited about what you do. As you learn new things, you have more to offer your clients — which helps with client retention and word of mouth referrals — but it also makes you more valuable because you are a joy to be around. You have a wealth of knowledge that is ever-expanding which makes you able to help any client that sits down in your chair. You aren't tired or bored, your energy is endless, as is your enthusiasm. In turn, people will be attracted to you and all that you know and have to offer.

If you stop learning, you'll stop growing and then you'll stop succeeding. Do you want to go to a doctor that hasn't been to school or learned anything new in 20 years? I don't think so. To be in the fashion industry is to be on the cutting edge. You are in the service industry as well — you're here to service your clients by helping them feel and look outstanding. The more you know, the better able you are to help them.

STEP 10. SELF-MOTIVATE

As you probably noticed from my story, I was a real self-starter. I didn't just "go to cosmetology school." I looked for opportunity everywhere and I took action. That meant getting a job cutting hair at the mall for experience, cutting all the hair I could get my hands on at the YMCA for peanuts and actually getting my hands dirty and legs tired at trade shows, doing cut-a-thons and getting involved in the community.

If there's one thing I know for sure, it's that opportunity rarely comes and sits down in your lap. And even when it does, we often don't recognize it. If you want to be outstanding you need to search for success, hunt it down, and grab hold. As you work to become booked solid, what opportunities can you take in order to get more clients, meet key people in the industry, experience as much as possible, and show the world that you are a success (or well on your way). Look around your community and see what you can find. Always keep your eyes open.

Remember, you and your own success are your responsibility. You need to keep that motivation level high. There will be hard days when it will be easy to throw in the towel and give up. Here's how I avoid them: keep a journal. Document all of your accomplishments and even document the challenging times and how you overcame them. Then, when you are having one of those bad days, look at the journal — let it help you remember how far you've come and how at other times, when things looked bleak, you rebounded. I still have my journal from when I was cutting hair at the YMCA more than 30 years ago. When I look at my journal, I can see the number of haircuts I did and what I charged for a haircut. Back then it was $3.00, basically just getting by. It wasn't about the money, it was about the experience.

Jimmy

WHEN I GRADUATED FROM HIGH SCHOOL, I WAS VERY interested in science. Chemistry was my thing. I was also very artistic. Both of these passions led me to hairdressing. When I was 23, I went to a cosmetology school called LaBaron and when I graduated, an instructor told me about a new guy opening up a salon in downtown Springfield. That new guy was Paul DiGrigoli, and I went to meet him and started working for him. That was 24 years ago, and I'm glad to say that I'm still with him today.

The important thing for me **then, became** my path to find **security when** things around **me are always** changing. My **answer is the** educational piece.

The artistic part of me and my talent for chemistry thrive on mixing colors, doing perms and helping people with problem hair (for example, taking certain medications affects their hair and I help them counter that). Anything to do with chemicals, I'm there.

Over the last 24 years, I've grown tremendously as a stylist and technician and the reason is simple: continuing education. In fact, the number one reason that I've stayed with Paul for this long is his passionate drive for education. He'd send me all over the country to New York City, Miami, Chicago, LA to learn new techniques. In doing so, he surrounded me with professionals, big names, the leaders in our field. The more I was around them and the more I learned, the more into the world I dove and the more motivated I became. We started out doing hair shows in a broken-down van; everything was done by hand and in pencil. Today it's all computers, jets and sleek settings — but learning and being the best stylist you can be is still the name of the game.

The other challenge working in one place for so long is change, oddly enough. The person who has been here with Paul the second longest next to me has been here for 8 years. It's hard to have such a good team and then watch it shift and change as people transition, get married, have kids or move. But, we started with four chairs and now we have 24 chairs. How could that possibly stay consistent? The important thing for me then, became my path to find security when things around me are always changing. My answer is the educational piece. I still go to at least four big shows every year, and when I come home my sales go through the roof. Learning, being around the top stylists, the energy, the talent — it pays off and keeps me moving up.

My success is a direct result of my hard work and the people that surround me. With Paul, it's never been like working for a boss, it's like working for a coach. He finds the best quality in each of us and he pulls it out — then he makes you go for it.

CHAPTER 8

Personal Development

What does personal development have to do with being Booked Solid? Everything... trust me. If you can't manage yourself, you can't manage anybody else.

UP OR DOWN?

When I think about personal development, I think of one of my favorite sayings: "If you're not growing, you're dying." The choice is up to you. Do you want to be on the upswing or the downswing? Do you want to be getting better or getting worse? I hope you'll choose the path that takes you right up to success.

If you want to grab onto that upswing, think quality, not quantity. It's not the hours that you work, it's what you put into those hours. Which is better, 10 mediocre haircuts where the clients never

The growing versus dying side of personal development isn't all about skill and technique, it's also about attitude.

PERSONAL DEVELOPMENT

▶ If you're not growing, you're dying

▶ It's not the hours your work... it's what you put into those hours that counts

▶ Psychology: **85%**

▶ Skill: **15%**

return, or one incredible cut that pretty much seals the deal that you'll have that client for life? Hairdressing is about quality, not quantity because individual clients don't care how busy you are, they only care how well you cut their hair — that's what keeps them coming back. If you *are* busy, but you aren't providing the goods, it's a good bet that you won't stay busy for long.

How do you provide quality? By honing your skills, of course. You can do this via observation, education, training and practice, practice, practice. Always keep learning, stay up to date on the latest fashions. It takes perseverance and sincere effort.

Still the growing versus dying side of personal development isn't all about skill and technique, it's also about attitude. For instance, if you are excited to learn, then it won't feel difficult at all. To choose growing, you need a good mindset and a positive attitude. If you are negative, it will pull you down until you can't grow anymore. You'll feel defeated and worthless, you'll lose your vision and your spark. By finding the good side of things, you'll have the energy and the desire to keep climbing higher. When I'm teaching a haircut to my students, I tell them if it feels uncomfortable, that means you're learning. If you can do it right away, it means you know it.

BUILDING CONFIDENCE: THE POSITIVE SIDE OF FEAR

Most people focus on the negative side of fear. Granted, there is something to that! It's important to realize that often it's fear that holds us back from success and from trying new things. It's fear of the unknown, fear of the outcome, even fear of total success, believe it or not! But, I want to look at the other side of fear, the positive side of fear. Sometimes it's good to be afraid and uncertain of the future because when we feel too safe, we get complacent. There's no need to move forward and we get stagnant. To some degree, a bit of fear and excitement keeps us searching for something better. I once heard that when you're about to start something new, you should be 90% excited and 10% scared. The more new things you try, the more risks you take, the more you will build confidence. Think of each experience — whether you failed or succeeded is a notch in your confidence belt. No, not a notch, but rather a step up the ladder.

BUILDING CONFIDENCE
- ▶ Break the fear and uncertainty
- ▶ OP & OPE
- ▶ Education (classes, DVDs, etc.)
- ▶ Learn through observation

OP & OPE

Interestingly, your path of personal development is affected highly by other people (OP) and other people's experience (OPE). It's how we learn as hairdressers — directly from others in schools and training, and indirectly through observation. You share your expertise and experience with your colleagues and they share theirs with you.

But you have to be selective when it comes to other people. You want to surround yourself with people that are successful, positive, hungry, and caring. If you want to get better be around people that are living at the highest level. People that aren't headed in the same direction as you are less likely to give you good information, they're less likely to have your best interests at heart if they're really looking out only for themselves.

PRACTICE MAKES PERFECT

You simply can't advance yourself if you don't take action. We learn by doing. If you want to instill new habits that will make you a better hairdresser and a better person, you need to practice and repeat the actions until they become second nature. This takes two things: passion and discipline. If you don't have passion, if you don't really want it, then you don't have a fighting chance. It's like your teacher telling you that you have to do your math homework, when all you're interested in is art. Meanwhile, you'll happily practice painting — even technique — all day. This is because the passion for painting is strong. As a result, it's easy for you to have discipline. You're willing to take classes, study different sorts of paints, even art history — because each of these trainings are related to what you love the most.

With hairdressing, it's the same. If you love fashion, people and cutting hair, you'll put the effort into learning new techniques and building a high level professional routine, and creating a "chair-side" manner that makes your clients feel great. The existence of your passion will make the discipline easy and effortless. And the practice-induced discipline will skyrocket your career. It's really a win-win situation. You just can't lose.

DISCIPLINE THE DISAPPOINTMENT

There's another side to discipline, and it's about not letting the bad days get you down. Obviously, I can't promise you that from the moment you read this book, everything will be perfect in your life. Just go back and read my story! There will be pitfalls, setbacks, obstacles and just plain old bad days when things don't go your way. But what you do with those hard times is totally up to you — and it makes all the difference as you move forward.

THE PAST DOESN'T EQUAL THE FUTURE

Just because a client wasn't thrilled with the cut you gave them yesterday, doesn't mean that everyone will hate their cuts today. If you focus on the mistake or the negative, it will affect your mood and your performance and, yeah, increase the chances that this will be another bad day. I say, don't focus on the mistake. Every day is a new day, and you have the opportunity to start over. Instead of focusing on the negative, focus on the positive.

Now, I know this is hard. Most people find the negative very alluring! Has this ever happened to you? Let's say you're practicing a new cut and your teacher gives you a critique that sounds like this, "You got the balance just right and the

DISCIPLINE THE DISAPPOINTMENT
- ▶ The past doesn't equal the future
- ▶ Perseverance outweighs the pain of regret
- ▶ Work on your weaknesses
- ▶ Don't look for what's missing

angles work very well for this face shape. I love how you texturized the bangs. Next time you might want to think about a weight line in the back."

Okay, now, what did you hear? The majority of people hear one thing, "I'm not comfortable with the weight line". Even though there were three compliments and the criticism wasn't even very intense, humans are hard-wired to pick out the one negative item and make it even bigger than it is!

PERSEVERANCE OUTWEIGHS THE PAIN OF REGRET

After receiving that critique, you have two choices. You can focus on the negative and beat yourself up about it which will cause your negative attitude to spiral down. Or, you can look at it as an opportunity. With a positive spin, you can tackle the challenge and learn or perfect new skills. The negative spin usually just leaves you feeling bad and avoiding that particular task like the plague. You can't grow that way. You have to reach for more, even when it's challenging. You must work on your weaknesses, it's the only way to make them better. Otherwise, they just consume you because they make you feel bad about yourself, and because you have to work to avoid them causing stress and anxiety.

DON'T LOOK FOR WHAT'S MISSING

That said, don't go searching for your weaknesses. They'll come up in due time when you are ready to handle them, but if you go looking for them, you will get distracted. It's always best to focus on the good stuff. Put your attention on the positive, the present, and what you do best. If you keep your focus there, you will feel good, act good, and do good. Your mood and attitude will make people want to be around you — colleagues and clients. You'll have high energy that will motivate you to learn more, do more, and be the best person you can be.

HEALTHY LIVING: EMOTIONAL HEALTH

When people think about health, they immediately go to the physical body, but don't forget about the mind and the heart. Take care of yourself by having fun, talking to friends, relaxing, and taking time off. You have to unplug to recharge. So leave work behind at the end of the day or on your day off and do things that make you feel good. Do you love to paint? Play soccer? Cook? Find the things that feed the *other parts* of your brain — the parts that aren't exactly tied to being a hairdresser. When you put all the parts together, happily, they make a positive person who's Booked Solid. If you don't have energy and you don't feel good, you have nothing. You never do your best work when you don't feel good. My philosophy on that is, "People who don't live well, don't feel well."

YOU ARE WHAT YOU EAT

What do your food choices have to do with being Booked Solid? A lot. When you eat junk food, you turn into junk. When you eat unhealthy food, you get an unhealthy body. Maybe you're very young and you can't see it yet, but it's happening.

I encourage you to take the other path. Feed yourself healthy food that will give you energy and make you feel and look good. First of all, you need energy to stand behind the chair all day and to interact with your clients in a happy matter. They don't want you falling asleep while their blond highlights turn into a bleached disaster, and neither do you! Second, you need to feel good or you'll drag through the day, have to cancel clients due to illness and you won't have any "umph" left to go that extra mile. Finally, in this business, it is important to look good. Would you go to a personal trainer that was overweight and out of shape? No way. So you need to take excellent care of your body and your hair. Take the time to make yourself look fabulous and flaunt your talents — be your own personal billboard.

Did you know that 85% of the people in this country are on prescription drugs? It astounds me, especially when these drugs are helping people remedy unhealthy behaviors! If you could just fill your body with the right kinds of fuel in the first place, you simply wouldn't need the drugs to cure what ails you. This is what I call a Chemical Diet. The biggest drugs we give each other everyday is what we put on our dinner plate.

When you take a drug, it creates a chemical reaction in the body. I like to think that the biggest drug is food. How you feed yourself during the day has a major impact on how you act, look, and feel. Change your fuel and you'll change your energy — it's that simple. Our digestive system takes the most energy from our body. Think back to last Thanksgiving; after the big meal, all you wanted to do is lie down. All of your energy was being spent digesting. When we eat food that is hard to digest (think fast food), our body struggles and there's not much energy left for the other things in life. Think about eating a big meal before bed — you might sleep for 12 hours and wake up tired. That's because your body never rested — it was trying to deal with the meal all night!

The late meal schedule is a pitfall for stylists. We work all day, running around without the time to eat or take care of ourselves. Then we get home at 8:00 or 9:00 pm and eat a big meal. We don't sleep well, wake up, and start the cycle of not eating all over again. It's just horrible for our systems. We need energy for our clients, both physical and emotional. Yes, I know that hairdressers are the fastest eaters in the world, especially on Saturdays. I mean we can put down a 6 inch sub in about thirty seconds, and you know what I'm talking about. How about when you go in the back room on a Saturday and someone says in the salon that your food is here. And when you go back there you see that it's half gone, or someone ordered you the wrong thing, but you still gobble it down anyway. Sound familiar?

I'm a big believer in eating water-soluble foods (like fruits and vegetables) and whole foods, or natural foods. In general, I stay away from the <u>3W's</u>: white sugar, white flour, white salt:

- Sweeten naturally with honey, maple syrup, or stevia.
- Use whole grain flours and eat whole grains; wheat bread is very easy to digest.
- Replace table salt with authentic sea salt which is packed with nutrients and better for your blood pressure.

I encourage you to take time to eat during the day. Bring a healthy lunch with you to work. Don't get to that point where you're so hungry but unprepared, that there's nothing but fast food on the horizon. By the way I still enjoy ice cream and snacks every once in awhile but in moderation.

EXERCISE

Just like eating well, it's important that you exercise for health reasons and for professional reasons. Physiologically speaking, you need to get your blood pumping — for overall health, weight management, stress release and other reasons. Professionally, you need the stamina to stand all day — cutting, shampooing, coloring, and everything else we do in a day. Just like with healthy eating, exercise will help you project the beautiful and strong image that will help you encourage people to sit in your chair and stay there.

The easiest form of exercise is walking. This is because it doesn't hurt! You can do it outside or on the treadmill at the gym and all you need are comfortable shoes, so it's super cheap. Of course, you can hit the gym to get your cardio and weight-training. But you can also get exercise by playing team sports like soccer, basketball, tennis and lacrosse — giving you the added benefit of hanging out with friends and teammates. By doing any form of exercise it allows for some great down time and really allows to organize your brain.

LEARN HOW TO CHANGE YOUR CONDITION

Hopefully, I've been clear about the fact that life will throw you some curve balls. Maybe there will be another stylist that you don't get along with, maybe the hours you work aren't your favorite. Whatever it is, you can change your reactions to whatever the "badness" is. It takes some work and dedication, but the other option is to be miserable, and as we all know, that won't help you to get booked solid.

I encourage you to break your habitual and negative patterns. For instance, if someone says something rude to you and you usually yell back, do the opposite. You could walk away or quietly say, "That wasn't very nice," and then walk away. Notice that when "bad" things happen and you react in your usual way, it just makes you more upset. Whereas if you do the opposite, you might feel okay. Do some experiments, see what happens. Always be proactive and not reactive.

Getting stuck in destructive patterns is like getting stuck on an escalator that only goes down...and goes down forever. I hear people all the time say things like, "I'm not a morning person" or "I could never be *that* successful" — but I think they can. I think that they have a belief that is holding them back. If you make an effort to get up at 7am every morning, have a good breakfast and go for a walk — you'll notice a change. First of all, you'll want to go to bed earlier at night making it easier for you to get up the next morning. Practice makes perfect and facilitates change — you'll be a morning person in 21 days. And you said you couldn't do it! Can you imagine what it would be like to start your day like that every day? Can you imagine the impact that you would make on the people around you? You know, I must say that whether I'm at my salon or school, or speaking nationally, or when I'm out with my friends, I'm very predictable and very consistent with my behavior. It's very important to be consistent.

This lesson applies to anything in your life. You can do or be anything that you decide to do or be. Break the pattern that says you can't, change your behavior, stick with it and soon you will be able to reach any goal. The pain of discipline outweighs the pain of regret, that's for sure.

TRY YOUR BEST AND BE YOUR BEST EVERY DAY

I know a day was good if I can honestly tell myself that I did the best I could do. Even if something goes wrong, it's never tragic if I gave it my all. Other people will appreciate this too, you know. You'll stand out — not necessarily because you do everything right and always succeed, but because people can tell that you gave 100% effort. No laziness, this — again — is all about passion and energy. Put yourself out there in order to win. Focus on what really matters instead of the things that don't matter.

MAKE DISCIPLINE A PART OF YOUR LIFE

These steps for healthy living will not work if you don't make the time for them. If you're going to implement change, transform your habits ,and add exercise to your list of to-do's, you'll need to set up schedules. Write down everything that you have to do every day and create a system to get it all done — not only will this help you achieve your goals because you're organized, it will also severely reduce your stress.

Without a schedule, you'll start every day with a chaotic list of things that you have to and want to do swirling around in your head. Chances are, you'll get overwhelmed and end up doing nothing! But, if you have a schedule that tells you what to do (e.g. 8:00 wake up and go for a walk / 9:00 eat breakfast), then you'll be able to successfully manage each of those tasks one at a time. Try it. I think your production level will go through the roof. You'll be on time and prepared for work — treating your clients like the royalty that they are — and you'll feel great, knowing that you aren't in a rush or overwhelmed, but, in fact, right on time.

REMEMBER YOUR ACCOMPLISHMENTS

You're doing a lot of good work here, I hope you know it. To make sure you do, take some time, maybe every night before bed or at the end of your week to acknowledge all that you've done. Even little things like, "I ate vegetables at lunch," or "I made it to the gym," or "I was fully booked today" — the list can go on and on. Perhaps every three to six months, you revisit your goal sheet. Believe me, you deserve a little round of applause, a friendly pat on the back from yourself. No matter how you do this, it's important that you mark things off your list, measure your progress, and see how far you've come.

Of course, your successes will serve as motivation for creating bigger and better goals for yourself. Let your accomplishments — big and little, day-to-day and year-to-year — fill you up, like fuel to boost you even further into the stratosphere.

CHAPTER 9

Motivation

THE POWER OF HIGH LEVEL MOTIVATION

Motivation. It's the fire that burns inside of you and propels you forward to be better, do more, and achieve everything you've ever dreamed. As a hairdresser, you need to be motivated to become Booked Solid and your motivation will rub off on your clients. You'll end up motivating them to try new things and to feel good. Motivation comes in many forms: education, music, art, food, people, events. Simply put: *If you're not moving forward, you're moving backwards.* The following are the main components for staying motivated and moving forward as you work to become Booked Solid.

My big question for you is, what do you want to do? Where are you right now? Expanding or standing still? What's holding you back?

PASSION AND ENERGY ARE EVERYTHING

Energy is the source, nothing happens without energy. And the more energy that we have, the more we can tap into our personal power. Think about energy like the gas that drives your car to success. Of course you don't want to run out of gas. Otherwise you'll find yourself coasting back downhill. You have to keep that tank full or you'll never make it where you need to go. And you have to think about using the right kind of fuel. If you put in good, then good comes out. If you put in garbage, then garbage comes out. High octane fuel is the key.

How many of you jump out of bed first thing in the morning and say, "Oh god! I can't wait to save the world, change everything around me! I can't wait for today!" The typical first thought is something more along the lines of, "Where's the coffee?" or "Not another Monday!" — and you continue to hit the snooze button.

Be passionate and positive about your work — the results will be extraordinary. You see, most people don't do well, because they don't feel well. And I don't mean just in the physical sense. People think sick is about sneezing, coughing, fever — but it's also emotional. When you get sad, stressed, anxious, angry or depressed, you don't feel well mentally, and quite often, you don't feel well physically. So, here's an important lesson: You don't have to wait to get sick to get better. If you don't take time now to be healthy, you'll be forced to take time later to be sick. But, if you do take the time now to be healthy, you'll stay healthy, productive and successful.

BE MORE VALUABLE TO THE CUSTOMER

If you can't manage yourself, you can't manage anyone else. If you can't take care of yourself, you can't take care of anyone else — your clients, especially. Again, we have to go back to your physical self because you can't work or get clients without it! You only have one body, you have to take care of it, all of it. There's an old saying, "If you don't look good, you don't feel good." It's old, but it's true. We're in the fashion industry, we don't only need to feel good to perform, we also need to look good.

The more alive you are, the more vibrant, the more you pay attention to the customer, give them impeccable service, the more solidly booked you will become. You don't go to a dentist that has rotten teeth or if you're trying to stop smoking would you go to a doctor that smokes. Same thing here, you want to go to a hairdresser that looks fabulous. It's easy when things are going well (or well enough) to get complacent, get lazy and take things for granted. But, remember this: your client is only your client when they're in your chair. Once their feet hit the floor, there's no guarantee that they'll come back. Make no mistake about it, your clients are observant — they know if you're on your A game or on your B game. When you're on your B game (or below), they'll leave.

It takes four visits to make a client a <u>loyal</u> client. During those appointments, you need to ooze positivity, trust, consistency, professionalism, and stellar technique. The greater you feel, the greater you can make your customer feel. Clients are coming in to look for help, they want you to take away their pain. Both the physical pain (bad haircut, bad color, chipped nails) and the emotional pain

HIGH LEVEL OF MOTIVATION
▶ Change your fuel and you'll create more energy
▶ Passion and energy are everything
▶ Be more valuable to the customer
▶ Master your business

(sad, out of sorts, low self-esteem, bored). But if you don't feel good, how can you make them feel good?

MASTER YOUR BUSINESS

After 30 years, I've realized that it's very hard to be all things to all people. I've proven to be a great leader, entrepreneur and technician. But, it is a daunting task to do them all at once. At some point in your life, you have to give something up. Fifteen years ago, I had to make the hardest decision of my life. I had to step away from the chair to make my business and my career what it is today. I made a choice to focus my efforts on being a national spokesperson for the hair industry, the head of my cosmetology school, and the owner of my salon.

I don't know where I'm finding you at this point. You could be a platform artist for a major player in the fashion industry or a booth renter, but whatever you do, you have to learn about what it takes to run a salon. Of all 350,000 salons in the U.S., a whopping 85% are not profitable — even though it's a 60 billion dollar hair industry. This is because people don't learn how to master their business. You have to decide specifically what your goal is and what you want your outcome to be. Five years behind the chair? Ten?

One of my stylists, Jimmy, has been working for me for 24 years. He's not interested in opening his own business. He makes great money and has great benefits as it is. Still, he gets pestered by his clients. They always bug him to open his own salon because he's an elite stylist and brilliant with color. And here's why he doesn't want to go out on his own and why you need to have clearly defined goals. If you see 60 clients a week and that's all you do and then you decide to open a salon, you have to know that your artistry will be diluted. You'll come across major distractions including, but not limited to, talking to salespeople, paying bills, hiring, firing, marketing and beyond. So now things will change. Sometimes hairdressers are too ambitious because they don't know what they're getting into as a salon owner. If you don't, you could set yourself back five years. If you're going to open up your own business, you need to know what's in store. Many people think they'll open their own business and suddenly have total freedom and personal time. False! Most salon owners admit they would do it differently if they had the chance. They wish they'd understood the big picture, they wish they'd had a map and a blueprint.

At one time, opening your own salon was a dream. After two or three years in the biz, your own salon has become a huge challenge, ripe with problems. The only reason is because you didn't prepare properly and there's a lot more than just having your name painted over the front door when you become an entrepreneur. Its invariably hard, hard work. So by being prepared you have less chance of failure.

Though it may sound like it, I'm not trying to dissuade you. I just want you to be prepared — so that you will be a raging success. I'm also telling you that, while it's possible to do a lot of things really well, there is a tipping point where you discover that you're trying to do too many things at once. The solution is to take stock and evaluate what your top priorities are. Choose them carefully and let go of the pieces that aren't necessary and important. Slim down your goals, be honest and fair. Then, go get 'em!

CHEMISTRY: THE INNER CIRCLE

Beyond skill, I think chemistry is an essential ingredient for any winning team. It's the chemistry that makes you the best salon ever. You have to have chemistry in your salon, it's critical for success. If you're just starting out and looking for a good salon to join, go to at least five of them in your area. Hang out in the reception area for a couple of hours and watch the interactions and rapport between the stylists, the stylists and the receptionists, the clients and the stylists. You want a place where it feels good and the people are happy and productive. Why? Because whoever you're surrounded by, that's what you'll become. This is a major component of growth and development, and the people that you work with become your Inner Circle. Make sure that some of these people have been in the industry for 10 or 15 years and that they've become masters in their chosen field. Not only will you learn from them, but you'll also become part of what they are: successful.

There are four major beliefs or feelings that must be in the inner circle:

- **Caring.** Do the people in your Inner Circle ask, "How are you?" If they see that someone hasn't had a break in a while, do they offer to do a shampoo or grab them a drink if they have a moment?
- **Respect.** This involves speaking nicely to each other, not taking tools without asking and being courteous. The Inner Circle should respect each others' beliefs, practices, space and person. This doesn't mean they have to agree about everything, by the way, they just need to honor their differences.
- **Harmony.** This is really a feeling you'll get. Are people stressed and frowning, bumping into each other and things like that? Are clients waiting impatiently? Or does everything seem to be moving like clockwork, is it smooth, are the sounds around the salon happy? Are the stylists having fun?
- **Self-Sacrifice.** If a stylist gets sick and has to go home, do the other stylists jump in and offer to take clients or can they do things without being asked?

You do not want to settle in an Inner Circle where there's anger, frustration, jealousy, animosity. In psychology they say that for every **one** negative person in the Inner Circle, **four** positive people are affected. So where do you want to be? The good Inner Circle creates growth, the bad one creates failure.

Look at it this way, you can't go to your garden and pretend there are no weeds. If you do, they'll take over your garden. I do an exercise every spring in my staff meetings, I ask my staff to come up and take a coffee cup and fill it with soil and plant some seeds in their cup. Then I ask them a major question, "What do you have to do now in order to grow this seed into a really beautiful blossom?" They come up with a ton of answers like water, sunlight, miracle grow, saran wrap to keep the moisture in, paying attention to it every day, talking to it, giving it positive reinforcement. Some of them take popsicle sticks and write "grow, grow, grow, get strong" and put it into the soil. They talk about encouraging and reinforcing positive behavior with words and actions. They talk about caring, respect, harmony and self-sacrifice.

My next question to them is, "Why would you treat the people you're around on a daily basis any different than the flowers?" I can't give you the Inner Circle you need to find, but I can give you the ingredients. This is no bull, it's very straightforward. So when you're venturing out, really pay attention at different salons and pick one with the right Inner Circle. If you get to the fork in the road, I encourage you to go right. Make the right decision. Why would that be any different when dealing with the people in your salon? You want to encourage

CHEMISTRY: THE INNER CIRCLE
▶ Caring
▶ Respect
▶ Harmony
▶ Self-sacrifice
Who are you surrounded by?

CHEMISTRY: THE WINNING CIRCLE
- ▶ Staying steady
- ▶ Being consistent
- ▶ One caring for the other

Beware of what you'll become

your people, not discourage. You want to give them positive feedback and catch people doing things right. Give a genuine compliment every single day.

Maybe you're stuck in a salon with a lot of negative people in it, maybe you don't want to leave because of fear of the unknown. Fear is the biggest thing that holds us back. I'm going to give you some insight to go to the next level. Did you know that we make decisions in a minute, a second, a heartbeat? Then you make the move. Most people think that decisions take a long time, but it's not the decision that takes a long time, it's the procrastination leading up to the decision, the over-thinking and over-analyzing. We can procrastinate for months, years, and never make that step. But you don't have to. You can make the decision right now.

There's a 49-year old student at my school. His whole life he wanted to become a hairdresser. He stayed in that job for 20 years, until one day, he got a pink slip, they had eliminated his job. So he said, "What's my dream?" And the answer was, "To be a hairdresser." He said 20 years later that this was the best thing his boss ever gave him. Sadly today, we don't have as many great leaders or mentors; people are often greedy and worried about things themselves, so much so that they can't help others. Even now, as a I write this book, our world is going through some very turbulent times, But sometimes this is the best time for opportunity, when things really get shaken up.

So my big question for you is, what do you want to do? Where are you right now? Expanding or standing still? What's holding you back? If you're on the fence, it's the worst position you can be in. I call it the "unresolved" — you're not in the game and you're not out of the game. Make a decision. Don't wait for your ship to come in, swim out to it.

CHEMISTRY: THE WINNING CIRCLE

If the Inner Circle is about a feeling or a vibe, the Winning Circle is about action. The Inner Circle has to be riding the good wave in order to get into the Winning Circle. We always want to be around winners. There is nothing greater than reaching your goals, when the salon you choose to work with or create holds major influence over your ability to succeed. The Winning Circle takes the components of the Inner Circle to the next level. The caring, respect, harmony and self-sacrifice can support and boost all of you into maximum achievement. The three main ingredients for the Winning Circle are:

1. **Stay Hungry.** Not for food, but for meaning, for what you want to become. Continually reach for your goals and dreams — and set new ones, higher ones, as you rise in your achievements. Keep learning, training, growing. Always have an appetite for more.

2. **Be Consistent.** It's easy to get complacent. If we don't stay consistent — in our technique, professionalism and motivation, we have a tendency to fall back a few steps. Those few steps can lead to deterioration of all we've built. Suddenly, we aren't Booked Solid. The action of consistent success and motivation is critical.

3. **Cohesion.** Have you ever seen those diagrams with the happy faces on the inside of the circle and that one sad face on the outside? The sad face is trying to coax the

happy people to the negative side. It would be easy to look at that sad face and dismiss it, even ignore it. But, to hold the Winning Circle together, you need to care about everyone in the salon — the other hairdressers, the boss, the clients. Can you help the sad face? Sadly enough, you can't change behavior. You can teach someone to perm, to cut, to color, but you can't teach someone their behavior. The salon owner that keeps those people on, mark my word, will see their business suffer.

BUILD THE WINNING CIRCLE: QUESTIONS TO ASK YOURSELF

- Who am I around?
- What are they doing for me?
- Where do they have me going?
- What will I become?
- How is it the major piece to your life puzzle?

Carlos

I'VE BEEN IN THE HAIR BUSINESS FOR 25 YEARS NOW—AND I love it. I actually got into it because of my mother, I'm a second generation hairdresser. And after hairdressing school, I initially went to work with my mom at her studio, but decided that the family business wasn't what I was looking for. I wanted to be successful—that's what I do know. So, I watched the icons in the industry and emulated them. I met Paul in 1989, back when he was a freelance educator for KMS. I trained at his Academy and listened to him teach whenever I could.

Paul told me that I had to **learn as much** as I could, that it **would make me** great, so I **took a public** speaking class at **Dale Carnegie.**

In 1990 I opened my own hair salon, and became affiliated with Toni & Guy by selling their product line exclusively. At the time, Paul was doing the show circuit and I had always wanted to be a platform artist. I was just in awe watching him speak and doing the shows—he was so motivational and inspirational, there was just something about the way he held himself. So, I told him about my aspirations, and he talked me into doing a show with him onstage for KMS. I thought I'd flop, but he was so supportive and he carried the audience naturally. I was hooked and that was the beginning of my career as a platform artist. Paul told me that I had to learn as much as I could, that it would make me great, so I took a public speaking class at Dale Carnegie. And, I kept working with Paul. He gave this one talk about the 12 Characteristics of a Champion Hairdresser, and to this day, I still share these 12 Characteristics with people and live by them as best I can.

In 1995, I sold my salon and moved to Dallas to work for Toni & Guy. I was there for five years, climbing the ranks until I became the Education Director. When the company decided to open up a salon and academy in New York City, they asked me to be the Personnel Director. We had a great run for eight years and then decided to shut down the salon and put all of our efforts into the academy. I became the Creative Director for both Toni & Guy and the academy. Today, my title is Creative Education Development Director, and I'm in charge of creative endeavors in the Americas, and I still do platform work (which I've never stopped loving) and travel the globe for T&G.

I've been very successful and Paul has been a major part of it. He inspired me from the beginning with his giving spirit, his passion for the industry, and his belief that you can ride this train as far as you want to go. He lives it and breathes it—he truly is a living testimony. I'm lucky to work with him and call him my friend.

Marketing is the pump and you have to keep pumping the pump. Once it stops, your business and your clients will stop.

CHAPTER 10

Marketing

MASSIVE EXPOSURE

This is one of my favorite subjects: Marketing. One of the most important components any hairdresser can indulge in is marketing. It's all about how you sell yourself as a stylist. Whether you're a booth renter, employee, or owner, marketing is the pump and you have to keep pumping the pump. Once it stops, your business is over, as are your dreams of becoming Booked Solid.

In marketing, your professional presence makes up about 85% of who you are. You need to create a marketing image for yourself and make sure it matches the image that you're trying to project as an individual, as a stylist, as a part of a salon. Your image and all of your marketing materials are like a billboard, and how that billboard looks, what it says, and how it's perceived by people that see it are critical for getting

The most powerful way to grow yourself, your clientele, and your business is to strive to be interested, not interesting.

MASSIVE EXPOSURE

▶ Business cards
▶ Networking
▶ Cross-marketing
▶ Internal/external

Booked Solid. Marketing has many components. Imagine a bike wheel, you have to have all of the spokes to stay balanced. Let's look at the spokes on your marketing wheel.

BUSINESS CARDS

Everyone needs to have a business card and you need to carry them with you at all times. You just never know when you'll happen upon someone looking for a great stylist. Business cards should be:

- Colorful
- Readable
- Graphic (with a design, logo or picture)
- Simple and to the point
- Memorable (a tagline is great for this and three words is all it takes, for example: Nike "Just do it," McDonald's "I'm lovin' it," Coke's "Coke is it," Budweiser's "King of Beers"
- Make the front of the card glossy stock for a little shine, but...
- Keep the back matte so that you can write next appointment information easily — include a spot for date, time, etc.

NETWORKING

Truly the most effective way to become Booked Solid is through networking. To network, you must manage your time so that you have time to get yourself out there, and you need to find out what's happening in your local community. This includes events at your Chamber of Commerce, YMCA, Women's Clubs, Career Days, professional groups, even wine tasting events, to mention just a few. And don't forget about informal networking at the gym, the dog park, the coffee shop (this is why you *always* need to have your business cards with you!).

The goal of networking is that someone should be able to identify you within 6 seconds after meeting you. That's the good impression that you have to make. Meet as many people as you can at the event, you just never know who will be a potential client or who will then talk to someone who might be a potential client. After all, the bald guy at the bar might have a wife who gets a cut, color and up-do once a month! Be aware if they seem like they could be a potential client themselves. The first thing I do, when I walk into a room is look at everyone's hair. Find someone with faded hair, color that is out of proportion or a hair cut that doesn't look so great on them — something that you could work with, show your expertise. For a good prospect like that, I'd spend 15 minutes talking to them. Use a soft approach! Never start right in telling someone that their hair looks bad, find the good things about their hair, talk about the vision you see, invite them to come see you. Be suave.

CROSS-MARKETING

The important concept of cross-marketing means targeting different audiences with your image as you brand your salon and yourself. Advertise on radio, television, postcards, magazines, direct mail, the internet, newspapers — town or free papers — show your image everywhere. You might not get a ton of clients from any of these ads in particular, but repetition is the key. The more people that are exposed to you, the more impact there is.

In the paper, place your ad in the left hand corner as studies show that's where our eyes go first. Make it visible by reversing the color of what they usually do in the paper (black background with white writing, for instance), and keep it clean and simple. Here's the hairdresser's advertising Rule of Thumb: clients will only come to you within a 10 mile radius. So focus your advertising locally.

Of course, advertising costs money, so you'll need a marketing budget. I recommend 5% of your gross sales. So, if you make $100,000 a year, you have a monthly budget of about $416 ($5,000 /12). You can either portion out equal amounts for each month or concentrate your marketing money during certain times of the year when you're less busy. For instance, you know you'll be busy during prom and wedding season and again during the holidays. So spend your marketing dollars during the slower months.

INTERNAL & EXTERNAL MARKETING

When I talk about internal, I mean your existing marketplace and clientele. If you work out of a salon, you probably have access to a computer that can tell you an amazing amount of information about your work situation. It will tell you how many men you have, women, kids, your request ratio (how many people request you), how many new clients you have, and it will break down your bookings by the service. Every salon should have this data and every stylist should use it.

You'll be able to identify your hot clients — those that have had some familiarity with you or the salon. It'll tell you the clients who have been to the salon in the last three months and those who haven't. These are the ones to really go after. One great method is to send them a handwritten postcard with a message like, "I haven't seen you in the last 3 months and I miss you! Come on in, we'll give you 20% off." You can also be creative with deal offerings. For instance, you could place a tent card on your station, put signs in the bathroom, the reception area, or on your mirror.

External marketing goes out to the public — those who may or may not have heard of you. It includes radio, television, magazines, newspaper and the Internet. Experience has shown me that radio advertising is more effective in the summer, while TV works better in the winter.

THE INTERNET AND SOCIAL MEDIA

More and more today, people are turning to their computers and iPhones for information and I encourage you to use this to your advantage. While, the internet allows us to have universal reach to people we would never normally meet, it also lets us meet people, find events, and advertise locally.

- **Website.** It's a superb idea in this day and age to have a website — either for the salon or for yourself. You can make it an electronic brochure that tells people the basics: contact, directions, services, etc. or you can make it dynamic and interactive with a blog.
- **Blogs.** If you like to write, a blog can be a great help to getting you Booked Solid. If people are searching the internet for a new hairdresser, when they type in, *"your town* and *hairdresser or salon"* you want them to find you first. When you write a blog, your website becomes much more attractive to the search engines because each blog post is adding new content full of words like: hair, cut, color, perm, salon, etc. on a regular basis. You could write a blog about hair and esthetic tips, or one about the life of a hairdresser. Either way, if you can provide value and information (with your words, pictures and even videos), you'll begin to create an audience and, more importantly, a relationship with that audience. They'll only want to work with you — because you'll be giving them so much and because they'll feel like they know you. They can even comment on your blog and ask you questions! You can also be featured on other blogs in

the neighborhood extending your reach beyond your audience and out to someone else's. For instance, maybe you want to highlight your favorite personal chef and s/he wants to highlight you.

- **Social Networking Sites.** Facebook, Twitter, LinkedIn, YouTube and more! I'm sure you've heard of them, right? Well, by using them and their status update options, you can get information out to your network quickly. You can also search for people in your area — incredibly important for hairdressers. Who knows, maybe you'll make a hilarious hairdressing video and it'll go viral. In the end, these sites just offer you a new way to network — and you don't even have to dress up! By showing pictures and talking about your interests, you become more than a business advertising blindly, you have the opportunity to really connect with people — even though it isn't face to face. **Don't forget:** always be professional, even on the Internet, *especially on the Internet!* You don't want to lose clients by posting drunk or naked pictures. People *will* Google you, make no mistake about that!

- **Local sites & advertising.** Every town has them and they're a great place to advertise, especially because if people click on your ad, they can go right to your website or blog and learn all about you.

- **Cost.** This is the best part! Marketing and networking on the Internet costs nothing but your time (which I do realize is precious). These days, you can put up your own site or blog for free or for as much as you'd like to spend on professional design. Internet ads do cost money, but usually less than print advertising and they're much more targeted.

So after all this, I must say that the best marketing tip of all is that if you do absolutely beautiful hair, you will become booked solid.

FOUR WAYS TO MAKE MONEY

1. Services

The more services that you can offer your clients, the better the chance of retention. If you do:

- 1 service, you'll retain the client 50% of the time
- 2 services, your retention increases to 65%
- 3 services, your retention increases to 75%
- 4 services, your retention increases to 80%
- 5 services, your retention increases to 99% or for life.

However, when a first time client comes in, I encourage you to work your way into it. Don't hit them with everything when they first sit down in the chair if they're a new client — you'll scare them! Imagine if your mother came in for a haircut and someone launched into all of the transformative things they were going to do to her, seconds after meeting her! Listen to what your client needs. Then, during that first visit, just do the haircut (unless they come in for something more specific). As the appointment ends, say, "I'd love to see you with some highlights!" When they respond positively, you say, "Great, let's book the next appointment for two hours..." With each new appointment, keep listening and helping your client feel outstanding. The services will build naturally.

FOUR WAYS TO MAKE MONEY
▶ Service
▶ Retail
▶ Repeat business
▶ Referrals

Client retention scale

1 service =	**50%**
2 services =	**65%**
3 services =	**75%**
4 services =	**80%**
5 services =	**99%**

2. Retail

Here's the Rule of Thumb for salon retail: always sell 18% in retail products in relation to how much you bring in a day in service sales. So, if you make $300 in a day, to sell 18% of that in retail, you would need to sell $54 worth of product. We all know that in the old days, salons really held the retail power as most brands were available exclusively to them. But at some point, high end products started showing up in the aisles of your local drug store. It's not the same as buying products in a salon, and you make the difference. Whenever a client sits in your chair, you educate them about the products and the benefits to their hair and look. You teach them how to use the products correctly. You help them protect their investment — color, hair health, nails, skin — the entire look.

3. Repeat business

Always prebook your clients before they leave the salon. Talk to them about how long their cut or color will last until they'll need to see you again. If you can, walk them to the receptionist and let her know that you need to see the client in about six weeks. You can even offer incentives, for example, "If you book today, we'll give you 10% off that appointment." Prebooking like this gives you control over your financial situation and your schedule. You aren't worried if people will call and book again, you know that it's already done.

4. Referrals

Referrals serve as your report card. As a rule, if you do one *good* haircut, your client will tell five people. But, if you do one *bad* haircut, the client will tell ten people. Oh, and you'll never hear from them again. Be consistent, be good at what you do and keep improving. Our business isn't static, it grows and changes with the times and you need to grow and change with it as well.

CONSTANT COMMITMENT

Derived from the Japanese word *CANI* which means constant and never-ending improvement. When you live by *cani,* you have continuous growth and advancement. You want to become known as an expert, on the cutting edge, always bringing the best, and always in the know. *Cani* is the way. Here are the four parts to *cani*:

Focus: Eyes on the prize, avoid distractions.

Action: Knowledge is nothing if you don't put it into action, have a plan and move through it.

Education: Continue to learn, become addicted to education.

Language: The words that you choose to speak every day — to yourself and out loud to others — are directly connected to your performance and your success. Negative language and thoughts will defeat you. Always use positive, confident and kind language. Always ask yourself, who is moving you everyday? Answer is, you are! That's right.

EXPAND YOUR INCOME

Increase your clientele, increase your business, increase your paycheck. The first thing you need is **vision**. Then fill your life with **health**, physical and emotional, and this will help you **grow**. Before you know it your **business** will be soaring and your **clientele** will build and build. Ultimately, you'll receive a huge **paycheck** — literally, of course, but also in terms of satisfaction and contentment. There's nothing like being able to give back and making someone feel outstanding.

CHAPTER 11

Ethics

GREAT WORK ETHICS

Make tough decisions

One of the strongest skills a cosmetologist needs to have is the ability to do a total transformation on a client, but it requires creativity and imagination on the part of the hairdresser. First you must understand that there is a very fine line between a client *loving* their haircut and *liking* it. That line is based on two things: how well you communicate, your skill level and really how you execute the service.

In terms of communication, did you really listen to the client, or did you go with your own agenda? Did you clearly explain what you were about to do and what the transformation would look like? In terms of skill level, did you ask them the knockout questions and are you ready, can you do this? The key is to really identify the client's needs.

Make sure that you give back more often than you take. You are full of experience and knowledge that will also help your colleagues.

The decision that you have to make — *should I transform this client?* You're working on another person, in a way that will literally change who they are. If a person leaves their current stylist it's usually because s/he refused to change the client because they're afraid and don't feel confident in their skill. However, most clients won't leave their hairdresser because they feel too guilty, even if they aren't getting what they want. If your client really wants you to transform them, to be creative and take a risk, then you need the certainty and the skill to commit to what the client really needs. To do that, I recommend continuing to develop your skills through education and to surround yourself with high-level hairdressers.

Do more than what you get paid for
Always overachieve. Remember, your client is only your client when they're sitting in your chair, so you have to go above and beyond to get them back. Don't just dabble as a hairdresser. Even if you're a part-timer, you have to go all the way when you have your scissors in your hand. Offer a color, a new nail treatment, make the client happy. Bring your favorite client a coffee, offer them a discount on their next up-do, provide a complimentary conditioning treatment. Rise to every occasion.

Maintain your growth
If you don't maintain your growth, you won't be valuable to the marketplace and other stylists will pass you by. The more you grow, they more you can be an expert or even the best in your field. I've found that it's easy to become successful, but it's very hard to stay at the top. The race isn't over when you become the best; you have to work steadily to stay at the head of the pack. How do you maintain your growth? Education, travel, observation, learning from others, taking risks, and doing new things. Keep challenging yourself. It's very difficult to stay even, let alone get ahead.

Work hard every day

If you talk to any successful hairdresser and ask them what their secret is, none of them will tell you they work 9 to 5. The best cosmetologists work hard, serving 12-15 clients per day. But, it's not all about time with your clients. I encourage you to work harder on yourself than you do on your job. When you take care of yourself by getting rest, having fun, eating well and more, then you have that much more to give back to your clients and the salon. Your health and life energy will become added value for all. I call this *stacking.* If you can improve on any of these parts of your life on any given day, your value will increase. If you can just improve 1%, the effects of that 1% will turn into 2%, the 2% to 4% — all the way up past 100%. The success really builds on itself. Watch everything that follows, financial success as well as freedom, flexibility and time. It will certainly bring great knowledge and value so you'll have much more to give away.

When you get a good night sleep, you wake up feeling rested and then take the time for a good breakfast. You get to the salon in a great mood and your clients feel it. You cut great hair and your clients rebook before they leave, which makes you so thrilled, that you have another restful night — and the pattern starts all over again. Of course, you might hit bumps in the road. But think how much easier it will be to pick yourself back up when you're at 50% or 100% than when you're at less than 20%?

If you're just starting out, it can be hard to see the promise of this success. But as you practice, you see how it works. When you started at school and you were working on a mannequin head, the first time you tried a 90 degree cut, you really had to work at it. You made mistakes, but the more you practiced and learned from those mistakes, the better you got. Then, when you tried a 45 degree cut, you still made mistakes, but not as many because you remembered what you'd learned from the 90 degree. The skills build, the confidence builds, and you're stacking. It works with life, and it works with technique. Step by step, inch by inch, you will get there.

Poor / good / excellent / outstanding

In order to be a Booked Solid stylist, you can't settle for being poor. Poor equals the door. Poor equals pain. You have no value to the marketplace with no skill. You also have no money and no future. Today, you can't even really get a good job. Good, these days really equals "average" and you'll be just getting by. I'm assuming, since you made the commitment to read this book, that you are an overachiever. And to me, that means you are excellent. Excellent in every aspect — in the practice of your skills, your professionalism, your personality, and the way you are with your clients.

Few people realize that there is another level: outstanding. When you're outstanding, you literally stand out from everyone else. In the Olympics, you can win three medals: bronze, silver or gold. Let's say there are ten people in the mile race. Third place wins the bronze, second place wins the silver and first place earns the gold. What about fourth place? The runners that come in fourth through tenth get nothing but the memory of the race, while the first place winner gets everything. Beyond the gold medal, they get recognition, a place in the history books, endorsements and new opportunities in life. The winner is outstanding. NCA is the National Cosmetology Association — and they are the U.S. representatives to Organization Modial Coiffure (OMC), which sponsors the OMC World Championships of Beauty. Are you ready to compete in the "Olympics" for hairdressers? How about the North American Hairstyling Awards (NAHA)? Where will you stand out? In your chosen niche? In your town? At your salon?

Peers and mentors

Ask your peers and mentors for their opinions, support, and guidance. When you're surrounded by good people — and you absolutely need to be — they help accelerate your skills, creativity, and performance in a short amount of time. It's contagious. Also, make sure that you give back more often than you take. You are full of experience and knowledge that will also help your colleagues. As soon as you've grown comfortable in this world, be on the lookout for a newbie that could use a kind word, some advice or tips — now it's your turn to be a mentor. I'm not sure that anything feels as good as helping others to succeed.

PERFECTION

Don't be hard on yourself

This is so important. We all know that every day is not perfect and that mistakes will happen, so give yourself a break. There is nothing good that comes from dwelling on mistakes, just a bad attitude and more mistakes because you'll be so distracted. Every mistake is an opportunity. Try to understand where you went wrong, accept constructive criticism when it comes, and then fix the problem. That is the best thing you can do. You can't take an error back, you can't erase it, but you can help solve a problem. And then move forward. Focus on 85% of the solution and 15% of the problem.

You can't please everyone

I know you'll please a lot of people, but there will be one or two that won't like you, your work, your salon, or their cut. One thing that I see is that no matter how hard you work to perfect your skills, things happen. For instance, people do change their minds about what they want. Or sometimes, they can make a request, but your interpretation of that request is different than theirs. The results are totally different 45 minutes later because of these different interpretations. Something to remember is that 99% of the time, what the client has is what they don't want. Curly haired people want straight hair, brown haired people want to be blonde, people with thick hair want theirs to be thinner, you get the picture. Listen not only to what the client wants, but what they don't want.

Even when you do your best and you think you've just delivered the best haircut in the world, the client might not like it. You can't beat yourself up. All you can do is listen, work hard, and fix any problems that come your way.

Monitor your physical and emotional outputs

When you first start out, you'll realize that being a hairdresser is hard, hard work. Of course, there's the physical part when you're on your feet all day and working with your hands in a very detailed, fine-motor way. It's critically important that you take care of yourself by eating well — hairdressers are notorious for being the fastest eaters with the worst diets in the world — and getting enough rest and non-work time. Do the opposite of your work day when you have time off, sit down to eat, take a walk, go somewhere quiet without other people.

But it is just as important to take care of the emotional wear and tear. We give advice and listen to our clients all day. In effect, our brains have to be turned on for 10-15 appointments per day. One way to help yourself is to listen to your clients more than you advise them. People want to be heard, so instead of trying to come up with new things to tell them or impress them with, listen to them, respond to them. Conserve your energy. Take short quiet breaks during the day and most importantly, have fun. Nothing uses more energy than being negative and grumpy. Laughter, smiling and joy will recharge you.

Hairdressing is just a matter of taste

Which makes it subjective, since people have different tastes. If you don't have great taste, you can't produce great results. Most hairdressers have a flair for decorating, design, fashion, and art. We're creative people by nature, we love the esthetic. If you exhibit your personal flair and taste, you'll attract people that agree with your taste and they'll be happy with the work that you do. If you dress in 80's preppy style, but then create punk haircuts, people will be confused and they likely will be unpleasantly surprised. In effect, you're a billboard for your style and your work.

Mirror and matching

When you're running the show, to have true success and get as close to perfection as you can, it's helpful to practice some mirror and matching and the client with the stylist. You want to match personality types so that there is support and harmony in the client/stylist relationship. Type A personalities are aggressive, forthright and good at asking for what they want. On the other hand, a Type B person is passive, easy going, and less decisive. If you can identify what type your client is by observing their language, dress, personality and voice and then match them with the same sort of stylist at your salon, everyone will be happier.

Just one example of how this can create difficulty for a stylist is, imagine two Type B's trying to order a pizza. They'd spend all day going back and forth, "You decide!" "No, you decide!" They'd never make a decision. Now imagine them trying to decide on what hair color to go with! Every pairing has some kinks to work out — even two Type A's can find conflict when they have differing ideas and Type B's can be virtually run over by a strong Type A. So match types as best as you can and remember that it's not always going to work out. It can get tricky — specifically when you, the stylist, don't have the tools and skills to deal with it.

Type A stylists:
- If your client is also a Type A, make sure not to take over and be sure to let the client exercise the level of control that makes them feel comfortable.
- But still be strong, Type A's get that and respect it.
- If your client is a Type B, soften your approach. If you make

**CONSTANT
COMMITMENT**
▶Focus
▶Action
▶Education
▶Communication

an aggressive transformation list for their first visit, you'll likely lose them.

• But help them make decisions, show them the options, and help educate them on the look that will be best for them.

Type B stylists:

• If your client is a Type A, practice standing firm in your shoes and holding your own. They'll respond well to you having opinions and not being wishy washy. They've come to you to be taken care of and pampered.

• But don't overdo it — remember they ultimately love to have control.

• If your client is a Type B, you also need to work on her confidence. Remember the pizza scenario I mentioned before? As the stylist, you'll need to help with the decision making and the action taking.

• But, you can also encourage your client to strengthen their will by prompting them to make final decisions about their look.

**Build a trusted network of peers
for support**

For advice, support and networking, your fellow hairdressers and friends in the industry are the place to go. Believe in them, and let them believe in you. Once you encounter this trust and form a strong network, your confidence will grow. Your experience will deepen as a result of your combined knowledge and so will your success. Knowing that you can draw on each other's experiences is truly priceless.

Make sure that you give back as well. In a solid network, the give and take must be equal to be sustained. Believe me, it will feel just as good, if not better, to help others as it does to receive support. Consider some factors to your participation in this network. If you need to go on a long vacation or maternity leave, will your peers at your salon take care of your clients? Your biggest fear will be that they'll take your clients — but that won't be their intention if there is trust. If you have a good relationship with your colleagues, they'll take care of you — in equal measures you take care of them.

Angela

I'M A BARBER AND I SPECIALIZE IN MEN'S HAIRCUTS. I WENT to barber school in 1979 and then worked for about seven different hair salons before I bought my own salon. Around this time, I became the Men's Styling Director for the Connecticut Hair Fashion Committee, a group that showcased the latest cuts and styles. For them, I worked a number of shows including the Connecticut State Trade Show, where I met Paul DiGrigoli for the first time. He was the guest artist at the show and after he watched me work, he told me that he wanted me to join his team because he was looking for someone who specialized in men's haircuts.

So, I started doing more shows with Paul in the mid-90's. He would showcase women's styling, and of course give his powerful motivation talks. I would do men's cuts and our other partner, Gretchen, would do up-dos and nylon hair. We traveled to shows all over the Northeast and I'd also work at Paul's Academy. Students would come in for the day and I'd teach them two haircuts. We also made and sold videos of our teaching. But, in reality, we didn't just teach the haircuts, we shared things that a lot of stylists didn't know how to do. I'd teach them in one day, what I learned in a lifetime — all of my shortcuts and tricks of the trade.

I believe that I was successful **because of my** love and passion **for my work,** because I kept **learning and** growing and **because I** surrounded myself **with people** like Paul.

The response was outstanding — to the classes and the videos. It was such an amazing feeling when the students would really get it, when you could see the lightbulbs going on in their minds and you could see the results in their work. Teaching is such a great gift. I always felt so good after our classes, so accomplished, like I gave something to someone and they could go somewhere with it — anywhere they wanted to go!

After 16 years, I closed the doors to my shop, ready to move on but full of satisfaction because I loved being a barber. I actually laugh when I think about that word, because it doesn't really describe what I did in my career. I created something bigger. I traveled, did public speaking, I was an educator. I believe that I was successful because of my love and passion for my work, because I kept learning and growing and because I surrounded myself with people like Paul. We're still great friends, you know. He's the real deal, he has an uncanny ability to light a fire under people. I consider myself incredibly lucky to have received some of his flame.

CHAPTER 12

Achieve Your Peak State

When you reach your peak state, you're able to work at a peak performance level. You feel stronger in body and mind because the entire physiology of *you* is involved. The impact is endless. When you hit this state, everything in your life improves. You change the way you move, the way you think, the way you feel. It's contagious and magnificent. People will be dying to get into your chair, to work with you, to be part of your world and to receive your gift. Be prepared for the intensity of the vibe you'll create!

PEAK EXERCISES

To achieve the peak state, you need to do peak exercises. This involves exercising your mind, body and emotions. It includes working on how you conduct yourself on a daily basis. What you eat is

As hairdressers, we're selling a look, a style and a cut directly. But we're also selling a feeling indirectly. We have the power beyond our technical prowess to make our clients feel outstanding.

what you are, who you surround yourself with is who you become, and how you act towards other people is how they'll act towards you. At the end of the day, what you do is what you get. And what you get is entirely up to you because you are in control of what you do, how you act, and who you are.

There's a specific bike that I like to ride at the gym. As you push the pedals, they don't turn fake tires, they turn the blades on a huge fan. The easier you pedal, the easier the fan goes offering little resistance, but the harder you pedal, the harder the fan goes offering more and more resistance. It's up to you how hard it is to pedal. On a day when you're tired, you can take it easy; and as you get stronger, and pedal faster, the resistance and strength building flows back at you naturally. You can't outgrow the bike as a useful exercise tool.

One of the coolest things about these peak exercises, is that they grow with you just like the bike. They work with you, and they're changeable — meeting you exactly where you need them to. How many times have you heard someone use the excuse, "That's just the way I am?" It's such a cop-out. You can work to change. Negativity is certainly a roadblock for many people. The more positive you get, the easier things are. However, most people change their language and they use words such as *someday* when I get a new job, *someday* when I lose weight, *someday* it'll get better. *Someday* leads to *nowhere*. And how about the word 'but'? *But* if I was a little older, *but* if I had a new car, *but* if I had more money, *but* if I had more time. So the words and the language you use have a significant impact on how you conduct yourself on a daily basis. It's called self-awareness.

As hairdressers, we're selling a look, a style and a cut *directly*. But we're also selling a feeling *indirectly*. We have the power beyond our technical prowess to make our clients feel outstanding. Here are the peak exercises that will get you to your peak state where delivering this feeling to your client is unavoidable; a vital key to becoming Booked Solid. You can get to your 100% peak state, let's break it down.

1. 7% equals the words you say to yourself. Like it or not, your self-talk has a huge influence on you. This 7% includes your habitual thought patterns, how you talk to yourself about yourself and how you think about other people and their actions. Is your self-talk positive, curious and interested or negative, judgmental and mean? Do you think, '*Maybe* I'll become booked solid' or 'I *will* become booked solid'? Do you think, ' I'm too tired to be nice to my clients today' or 'Making my clients happy today will make me feel so good'? Do you look at things as a problem or a challenge? **The exercise is to practice thinking positive thoughts, talking to yourself with kindness and encouragement and choosing words like "'will," "want to" and "I know I can" as the rule, not the exception.**

2. 38% equals your voice quality, tonality, volume, and the feeling behind your words. This time we're not talking about the voice in your head and heart, but the voice you speak out loud with. This is the expression of your thoughts. And not only do you hear it, but it makes an impression on everyone around you. It can be the difference between someone wanting to rebook with you immediately (if you're positive, upbeat and problem-solving) or never wanting to sit in your chair again (if you're a downer, nasty and unpleasant). **The exercise is to listen to how you talk to people and make changes towards positivity and kindness, if necessary. Practice the old saying *if you don't have anything nice to say, don't say anything at all.***

3. 55% equals how you move your body and your facial expressions. Your physiology can increase your level of energy and passion. Notice the messages that your body is sending. Do you look down when meeting people or do you meet their eyes? Do you touch people easily when you

talk or fold your arms defensively over your chest? Does your face habitually carry a smile or a scowl? **The exercise is to open yourself up and be light with smiles and easy movements that invite people to engage with you comfortably — let your joy and energy radiate. Your body and mind connect.**

Notice the progression of the exercises. The main piece is about your self-talk, what's happening in your own mind — you're starting with yourself. When you've turned your self-talk positive, it will be that much easier to talk with joy, kindness, and loads of energy. Finally, it will require little work on your part for your body to act out all of this greatness. Self-talk influences communication, which influences the way your body reacts. When you learn to transform your self-talk, everything else will fall into place naturally.

Love What You Do & Expand Your Happiness

I believe that the ultimate outcome in life is to EXPAND your happiness. To me, that means making everything better, *everything*. As you read this book, I hope you noticed that I didn't just talk about styling and esthetic techniques. I didn't tell you that it was all about marketing or who you know. I didn't singularly stress your professionalism or your networking skills.

What I did do was tell you that the road to becoming Booked Solid is paved with all of these stones and more. It's a holistic approach and it invites you to be well-rounded, thorough, and complete:

- Improve and perfect your technique and skills
- Always do more than expected
- Expand your service offerings
- Get better not bigger, everyday
- Be creative

As you reach your goals and improve yourself, you will find joy. You'll feel good about yourself and that confidence and satisfaction will just overflow into every area of your life.

- Surround yourself with GPs, great people and GCs, great coaches
- Learn, learn, and then learn some more
- Network like crazy
- Market in a massive way
- Take care of your body
- Take care of your emotional state
- Exercise, sleep and eat well
- Have fun, lots of it
- Always act like a professional
- Showcase your style with your personal look
- Make your clients feel outstanding
- Go the extra mile (or two)
- Become an exceptional hairdresser, mother, father, sister, brother friend, mentor, etc...
- Peak exercise, don't do things once in a while or when it's convenient, make it a must.

Here's the good news. Since there isn't only one key, you have the ability to lean a little on the things that come easy to you. Maybe your color technique isn't the greatest in the world, but your cuts are astounding, as is your energy, your marketing ability and your rapport with your clients. Maybe you don't feel comfortable at networking events, but you come up with popular promotions, you've surrounded yourself with outstanding people, and you pride yourself on your diet and exercise regime. Do you get it? You don't have to be perfect in every aspect here! You do need to try your best in each area, but there are so many places to work and excel, that if you're a bit slow in one place, it likely won't hurt your overall performance.

As you can probably tell, I'm an overachiever. I do everything at 200%, full throttle. If you're like me, you'll love this multi-faceted approach, because it means that you're never done.

There's always a new goal, a higher goal, to reach for. If you feel you've perfected your marketing skills, work on your wardrobe. If you feel confident in your waxing, work on your up-dos. When your professional life is going well, work on your personal life and your hobbies. I've found that when your business is doing great, your relationship is usually in the toilet and when your relationship is doing great, your business is in the toilet. It's very important to become centered and balanced. Don't tip the scale one side or the other. The minute you think everything is going great, is usually when the crap hits the fan. This is something that I had to learn the hard way.

If you're not like me, and you like to take things a little slower, this approach still works. Simply focus on your strengths first, get them solid, and then branch out into less secure places until you feel comfortable. Don't feel like you have to do everything all at once — the most important thing is that you feel good — because good begets more good. And the people around you will catch on to your good feelings. They'll want to be around you, work with you and sit in your chair because it feels great and relaxed to be there. If you're trying to do everything in your power to become Booked Solid, but you're driving yourself insane with worry and fear, you might look good on paper, but you won't feel good to the people around you. It's the people who are the most important — yourself included.

Now, here's the next part. As you reach your goals and improve yourself, you will find joy. You'll feel good about yourself and that confidence and satisfaction will just overflow into every area of your life. The happier you get, the better things will get. And even when you hit roadblocks, you'll be on such an upswing that they won't be able to knock you down too far. Not to mention the fact that you'll have the tools, experience, and network to help you through those hard times.

Remember what happened to me? I lost seven trusted, talented stylists and 49% of my revenue along with them overnight. If I hadn't been standing on my hard work, my technical expertise, my history, my reputation, and my network — and if they hadn't been so rock solid — everything would have crumbled beneath me. But I did have all of those things and they were incredibly strong, so I didn't fail. I thrived. In retrospect, I'm able to see that what happened, while it was very uncomfortable at the time, it was one of the best things that ever happened to me. It made me really think about what was important, refocus and go after my current goals with even more passion and verve. The drive that I got from this experience pushed me right over the top and it even made me even stronger.

At the heart of it all, I find joy in what I do. I love being a hairdresser and I love working in the hair industry. I love being en entrepreneur and I love giving back. I've been told that it's contagious. My chair is always occupied, so is my School of Cosmetology, and so are my seminars when I speak across the country. Sure the haircuts are good, as are the education and the information when I talk to groups. But what's really crucial is that my love for what I do shines through. I truly hope that you love what you do as well. For me now, it's all about appreciation and contribution. What inspires me and gives me intense motivation is to see every student that comes through my school and all of my employees excel to the highest level.

This book tells you how to become Booked Solid, but the same steps, the same building blocks, the same *recipe* also tells you what everyone (no matter the profession) wants to know: *how to live well and love what they do*. I know how, and it's written throughout this book. If you love what you do, then it will never feel like work. So, if you truly love what you do, you will never work a day in your life. You'll wake up every morning with a smile on your face. You'll enjoy the day, and you'll go to bed at night knowing that you gave your all to yourself and to those around you.

Can you think of anything better than that? Thirty years later, I can't, and I wouldn't dream of choosing any other life.

So, don't forget. This is all up to you and it's all in reach. I know that you can succeed and be Booked Solid. Just work hard, take care of yourself, love what you do and expand your happiness...expand your entire LIFE!

I'm still doing the same thing that I was doing thirty years ago. However, it's certainly at a different level and the amount of experience and knowledge that I've gathered over the years has given me many gifts that I can now give away. I'm talking about being able to give back in a **massive** way, not in a little way. When you gather those gifts it takes you to bigger and better heights than you ever could've imagined.

The game is easy. I want to thank you for reading. I hope I opened your mind and made you aware that you probably are doing better than you thought — and if not this will be a fresh new start. It's never over until you decide to do something different! I really want you to pull the best out of this book and apply it to your current situation. Without question I know you can bring yourself to the next level personally, professionally and financially.

I feel that maintaining your momentum is the name of the game. If you found that this book helped to move you forward in your personal or professional life, I'd like to hear from you. You can email me or maybe I'll see you at a seminar at some point.

One other thing, I hope I earned your respect. I certainly hope that this book has given you some insight, some tools and skills to help you become Booked Solid — not only in the salon but also in your life. Booked Solid doesn't just mean that your chair is always full, it means becoming a better person in every aspect of your life, it means having a full and joyful life. I wish you prosperity, health and happiness. Always live and love with passion.   — Pauly D.

Acknowledgements

Not only is a hairdresser without clients just a guy with scissors, but a hairdresser without his family, friends and community is just a guy with scissors. So this book is dedicated to the following people:

The DiGrigoli Artistic Team of DiGrigoli Salon — you all make DiGrigoli world go round.

My devoted executive assistant Jessica Stewart — your level of loyalty is truly uncommon and appreciated.

My students — watching you learn, create and excel lights me up as much as it does you.

The instructors of DiGrigoli School of Cosmetology — for leading and guiding each and every student.

In memory of my dad and brother Carmen — for all of our happy memories.

My Mom — for all of your unconditional love. Your love is my strength and has fueled my passion for life.

My brother Stephen and my only sister Sandy — for your constant love, interest, insights, and purity of soul.

My brother Robert — your outlook on life and leadership ability inspires me. You always seem to amaze me with your intelligence, capacity to love, and kindhearted spirit. Thank you for reading every word to make my book what it is.

My Uncle Lou — you have always been there for me with continuous love, inspiration and knowledge.

And finally to my daughter Dinnea, the light of my life — my wish for you is that you will pursue your dreams, remain devoted to your vision and live your life with passion. Always do more than what is expected. If you discover what you love to do, you will never have to work a day in your life. Love always and forever, Dad.